C000089394

Gifts & Books

Gifts & Books

From Early Myth to the Present

EDITED BY

Nicholas Perkins

BODLEIAN
LIBRARY
PUBLISHING

Contents

Domina
KATHARINA SANDYS
VXOR *Edwini Sandys*
DE LONDON MILI͞
TIS, DONAVIT. XX.
LIBRAS QVIBUS EM
PTI SVNT LIB.
SEQVEN͞
TES.

Octo volumina lingua Chinensi. f͞.

Vlysses Aldrovandus de reliquis animalibus
exanguibus. f͞. Bon. 1606.

Leon. Lessius de Iustitia & Iure. f͞.
Par. 1606.

Annib. Scoti Comment. in Scotum. f͞. Ro. 1589

Photÿ Bibliotheca Lat: cum Scholÿs f͞.
Aug. Vind. 1606.

Dan. Tossanus in tres Evangelistas. Mat.
Luc. Io. 4͞. Han.

Obeliscus Vaticanus Sixti. v. Pontificis. 4͞.
Ro. 1587.

Salustÿ Opera ex recognitione Gruteri. 8͞
Franc. 1607.

Zoroastri Tinelli Mulicus Consolvens

4͞ Sen. 1605.

Histoire vniverselle des Indes Orient. & Occi
dent. per Witefliet. & Ant. M. f͞ Dovai. 1605.

Indiæ Orient. pars 7ª autore Gerardo Aetbus.
1606.

Casp. Bauhini Theatrum Anatomicum. 8͞
Franc. 1605.

Io. Passerotÿ Orationes, & Præfationes. Idem.
de Literarum inter se cognatione. Ejusdem. Ka
lenda Ianuariæ. Ejusdem Oeuures Poetiques
8͞. Par. 1605.

Rod. Gualteri Archetypi Homiliarum. in.
Lucam. 8͞. Tig. 1605.

Hen. Arnisæi Doctrina Politica 4͞ Franc. 1606.

Indagatio definitionis Logicæ Hor. Cornachini.
4͞ Par. 1605.

Il Mundo Magico di Cæsare della Riviera. 4͞
Mil. 1605.

Gio. Nic. Doglioni del Theatro vniversale
de Prencipi. 2. vol. 4͞ Ven. 1606

Iac. Lectÿ Editio Poetarum. Græ. veterum.
f͞. Aur. 1606.

Hispaniæ illustratæ Io. 3. f͞ Franc. 1606.

Eusebÿ Pamphili Thesaurus temporum cum.
Castigat. & notis Ios. Scaligeri. f͞. Lugd.

Florilegium Philosophicum. Abrahami de

Acknowledgements

A huge amount of work stands behind a book such as this. The contributors and I are grateful to everyone involved in bringing it together. Special thanks go to Samuel Fanous, Janet Phillips and Leanda Shrimpton at Bodleian Library Publishing for supporting the idea and working with me from initial plans to final product. Many thanks to Sarah Coatsworth, Emily Brand, Susie Foster, Dot Little and the whole design and production team. This book has developed alongside the *Gifts and Books* exhibition in the Bodleian Library in 2023. It has been a pleasure to work with Madeline Slaven, Sallyanne Gilchrist and the whole exhibitions team, who have brought to the project creative ideas and practical help. Numerous curators in the Bodleian have answered queries, discussed materials, and given their time and expertise generously, including Alessandro Bianchi, Gillian Evison, Francesca Galligan, Martin Kauffmann, Rachael Marsay, Catherine McIlwaine, César Merchan-Hamann and Alasdair Watson. Paul Collins and Eleanor Standley at the Ashmolean Museum have also been very helpful. Much of the work on this book took place during Covid-19 lockdowns or restrictions, which made access to materials in libraries and museums complicated, and so I am especially grateful for the curators' generous help at a time when we were all stretched. Finally, many thanks for the vital financial support from the University of Oxford, the Faculty of English and St Hugh's College, Oxford.

Foreword

The Bodleian Library has always been constituted and transformed by gifts. These range from the volumes donated by Humfrey, Duke of Gloucester, in the fifteenth century, and still preserved in Duke Humfrey's Library at the heart of the Bodleian's site; to modern archives, such as those of the Anti-Apartheid Movement and of Oxfam; to the papers of writers and artists, including Bruce Chatwin, Alan Bennett and Shirley Hughes. Gifts not only of books but of electronic materials, photographs, and, of course, money to support our work, are all vital to the continuing development of the Library that Francis Bacon, sending Thomas Bodley a copy of his *The Advancement of Learning*, described as an 'Ark to save learning from deluge', as Felicity Heal describes in her chapter here.

I am therefore delighted that this book both celebrates and reflects on gifts and books. Its extraordinary range in time and space demonstrates how deep the relationships are between gifts, exchange, storytelling and the written word, from ancient myths that straddle languages and cultures, to recent books for young readers which continue to show how acts of giving make a difference – not only within their powerful fictions, but also by shifting larger narratives and expectations. In between these poles, the contributors help us to encounter magnificent and striking books from and beyond the Bodleian's collections: gifts for or from monarchs; intimate love tokens; the Victorian passion for Christmas books and annuals; and the birth of the book token. They also discuss the complex and often destructive potential of the gift as part of oppressive histories, including

that of the transatlantic slave trade, while showing how previously enslaved people shaped their own stories of liberty and dignity. The Bodleian's collections allow us to study such histories, but also place a responsibility on us to acknowledge how some of its own books have been given, seized or traded through war and empire. Maria Sachiko Cecire's chapter tellingly shows how contemporary fictions provide models for understanding and transforming these questions through new kinds of gift exchange.

Throughout this collection, the value emerges of encountering books as individual objects, with their own histories and trajectories – whether specially designed as a sumptuous gift, or preserving more modest evidence of exchange and pleasure. As Inge Daniels's reflective contribution suggests, one of the tasks of an institution like the Bodleian is not only to preserve books for the future – saving learning from deluge – but also to share as widely as possible the knowledge and creative energy that they continue to yield. This volume, alongside the *Gifts and Books* exhibition with which it is connected, opens up our extraordinary collections to just those wider encounters – gifts both of pleasure and of insight that I hope you will enjoy.

Richard Ovenden OBE, Bodley's Librarian

adiuuan'
loria
ntau sancti
fiat
nunc et se
sculoum
en
sita. impl
quetu circa
Memeri
q; nostri
ex illibata

Introduction

Nicholas Perkins

> I sometimes feel as if there is a great chain of stories that
> links us all through the ages. And each link in the chain is
> a gift received and passed on in turn.
>
> S.F. SAID[1]

Knowingly or not, you are probably an expert in gift-giving. You might
even be weighing up this book now, wondering if it's a suitable present:
assessing its value, its colourful pictures, its promise of knowledge and
pleasure, or how it would nurture a friendship with the person you
might give it to. Perhaps you are that very recipient. Exchanging gifts is
fundamental to human cultures, though it comes in so many guises and
with so many stories attached that thinking about gifts inevitably makes
us wonder what varies over time and space, and between people, as well
as what is shared. We might also ask what currents of belief or habit
flow around an individual moment of giving – even one that's small or
spontaneous. Gifts can start or develop our relationships in sometimes
surprising ways, but what is the interaction between that dynamic moment
of giving and the larger pattern of exchange? These are what Yunxiang Yan
calls the 'individual gift' and the 'collective gift', and what Marcel Mauss
famously analysed as a 'system of total prestations' (or obligations).[2] Can a
gift ever escape the clinging tendrils of self-interest, or the expectation of a
return, and should that matter?

Books and other written forms create a rich avenue to explore these
questions. They can be costly gift objects in themselves that perform subtle
dances of generosity and hierarchy: rewarding some and excluding others,
imposing burdens as well as generating delight. But they may also be modest
or personal – a book enjoyed and then shared with a friend, or even a gift
tag that turns a mass-produced commodity into a meaningful present. The
gift is not inert; it produces a surplus that prompts us to give in turn, while
something of the giver inheres in the thing that's given. Mauss used the
Maori word *hau* to describe this effect as a 'spirit' of the gift.[3] That surplus

0.1 This gorgeous Epiphany scene
from a book of hours (a medieval prayer
book) shows how gift-giving brings
humans into contact with the divine.
Reversing earthly hierarchies, the first
Magus has taken off his crown, kneeling
before Mary and Christ to offer his
gold. The domestic scene behind them
and the stable's damaged roof remind
medieval viewers how the gift or grace
of the Incarnation touches their fallen,
ordinary world. Oxford, Bodleian Library,
MS. Auct. D. inf. 2. 11, fol. 81v (France, 1440–
1450; illustration by the 'Fastolf Master').

is captured in many of the books and objects we discuss in the chapters that follow – from ancient Sumerian tablets to early book tokens, and from magnificently illuminated medieval manuscripts to contemporary stories for young readers. In addition, books are often not just gifts, but imagine or enact gifts too. Writing has been used since the earliest times to record acts of giving, and to tell stories about exchange, generosity and reciprocity. So in many cultures, books have become a powerful means through which people tell one another about the power of giving, and its risks. Stories act on their listeners or readers as gifts too: they bring something to us, often more than we bargained for, they expand and nurture our relationships, and they urge us to share them in new acts of telling, new moments of giving.

Each of the following chapters approaches these questions from a different standpoint, illustrated mostly from the Bodleian Library's extraordinarily rich collections. Chapters 1 and 2, by Francesca Stavrakopoulou and Camillo A. Formigatti, investigate the relationships between humans and gods in early myths and religions, recorded in Sumerian, Hebrew, Latin and Greek, and Sanskrit. They show how objects and stories engaging with sacrifice, generosity and belonging helped to order social relationships, warn against false gifts, and offer a model for believers aspiring to knowledge and wisdom. In Chapter 3 I explore how gifts and books are entwined in medieval culture, from royal and divine donation to intimate exchanges between lovers. The language of desire is shared across these spheres, and acts of giving can overcome barriers of power, imagining a donor coming into the presence of God – as in the story of the Magi giving gifts to the infant Jesus (figure 0.1) – or a poet within earshot of a prince. Gift can quickly become bribe, however, and while medieval writings celebrate generosity, they frequently satirize its corruption. In Chapter 4 Felicity Heal shows how the social structures of early modern Britain revolved around give and take, including books, advice, food and hospitality. Royal courts, such as those of Henry VIII and Elizabeth I, were sites of intense scrutiny and anxiety about giving, but in other contexts too, such as family relationships and education, understanding how to give, receive and reciprocate was both a challenge and a creative spur.

By the nineteenth century the illustrated gift-book was developing as a form, especially associated with Christmas. Fictional protagonists such as Meg, Jo, Beth and Amy in *Little Women*, or Scrooge in *A Christmas*

Carol, helped an expanding readership to negotiate the dilemmas of the market and the pleasures of giving. Faith Binckes discusses these developments in Chapter 5, showing how they gave rise to innovations in writing and bookmaking, including the development of book tokens, which promoted the gift of reading as a social aspiration, and claimed to ease the problem of present buying (figure 0.2). Wider access to books changes but does not remove the question of who takes part in exchange, and on what terms. Earlier I said that qualities of the person giving, and the dynamic energy of the gift, can inhere in a gift object; but, while the gift may grant a kind of personhood to objects, people have also been exchanged or treated as property, most shockingly in the form of slavery. Chapter 5 also discusses dramatic narratives of escape from enslavement, by Olaudah Equiano and William and Ellen Craft, who describe the horror of being treated as disposable objects, and their determination to create their own stories, and make their own relationships. In Chapter 6 Maria Sachiko Cecire shows how books for young readers are intimately bound up with the gift relationships between adults and children, and with ideas of childhood as a kind of gift itself. From fairy tales to fantasy fiction, stories for younger readers feature crucial moments of giving or powerful gift objects, and teach or enable those readers to understand their own capacity to give and exchange. They can revisit traditional narratives of service and sacrifice, but can also reshape or challenge those traditions: imagining, for example, a swallow and a stone prince falling in love, or that two Black children can go to Windsor Castle with gifts to free the ghost of a colonial wrong.

Throughout this volume, our discussion of the striking and beautiful items that help tell these stories is shaped by the way that anthropologists have investigated the gift as a 'total social fact' that regulates and enriches relationships between people, while also standing in complex relation to commercial exchange.[4] Chapter 7 is a reflective and personal essay

0.2 The inside pages of this advertisement leaflet claim that books are 'the one gift that is always welcome and is never judged by its mere cash value'. Early book tokens tried to retain some of that mystique alongside their convenience, and to appeal to a range of readers – though this artist's idea of 'everybody' and their caricatured reading habits is very much of its mid-twentieth-century time. Oxford, Bodleian Library, John Johnson Collection, Publicity Box 11.

by anthropologist Inge Daniels, using four pictures as starting points to explore how we can understand giving in the contemporary world, including gifts of books, cups and shells, and how modern economic structures interact with our altruistic ambitions, for example in charitable aid. She asks how we might nurture altruism in the public sphere; one example comes from the community responses to Covid-19, another from public spaces such as parks and libraries. Can places and institutions like this help unlock the benefits that come from interactions that are not (directly) marketized, if access to them is truly broad? I will finish this Introduction with a gift-book that intervenes in that very debate.

In 2011 the Poetree, a sculpture shaped from paper, and growing from a book, was delivered anonymously to the Scottish Poetry Library in Edinburgh (figure 0.3). It was the first of ten such sculptures, each intricate, beautiful and charged with meaning, mostly donated to cultural institutions around the city, including the Scottish Storytelling Centre and Edinburgh's Central Library.[5] The Poetree is a gift-book that honours the gifts of writing, reading and enjoying books. Its form puns on a phrase by polymath Patrick Geddes (1854–1932), 'by leaves we live', which is carved on the threshold of the Scottish Poetry Library and became its Twitter handle. The sculpture also includes a poem by Edwin Morgan (1920–2010), whose archive is held at the Library; his 'A Trace of Wings' is included on strips of paper that fall into a gilded eggshell – another image for the gifted process of receiving, fostering and giving back that characterizes poetic making. Morgan's poem is itself a tribute to the Northumbrian poet Basil Bunting (1900–1985), playing on his avian surname in a series of eight riddling descriptions of buntings, ending with 'Basil Bunting   the sweetest singer; prince of finches; gone from these parts'.[6] The accompanying card from the sculptor described the gift as 'in support of libraries, books, words, ideas', pointedly defending open access to public goods that can sometimes be taken for granted, or belittled as luxuries.

This book is indebted to the books, words and ideas housed in the Bodleian Library, using them as a basis to encounter gifts and the stories they tell across continents and centuries. Even if you have paid good money for it, we hope that you will read with pleasure, and in the spirit of the gift.

0.3 In March 2011 a book sculpture (later called the Poetree) was anonymously left in the Scottish Poetry Library in Edinburgh. Its accompanying note explained that it was given 'in support of libraries, books, words, ideas'. Scottish Poetry Library. Photograph copyright Chris Scott, 2012.

Chapter 1

Gods, Gifts and Writing in Ancient Religious Imaginations

Francesca Stavrakopoulou

'I fear the Greeks, even when bringing gifts!' In Virgil's *Aeneid*, a Trojan priest eyes a supersized wooden horse with suspicion and dread. Why would the enemy Greeks abandon their ten-year siege of Troy, leaving only an astonishing gift at the city's walls?[7] The answer, it is soon revealed, is that the enormous horse is an offering to the gods – and thus a powerful ritual object, demanding reverent Trojan care within the very citadel (figure 1.1). But this, of course, is a falsehood. And bringing the horse into the city proves disastrous. When night falls, the Greek warriors hidden in the horse's belly spill out. The city burns as its inhabitants are slaughtered.

Composed in the first century BCE, Virgil's Latin verse retelling of the Greek myth about the Trojan War has become a 'canonical' text of Western cultures, rendering proverbial its warning about Greeks bearing gifts. But the Trojan Horse is more than a cipher of *human* deception. Expanding on older versions of the myth long circulating around and beyond the eastern Mediterranean, Virgil's portrayal of the wooden horse is woven into a wider story in which the gods are often as unpredictable, and devious, as humans. Indeed, in the *Aeneid* the priest Laocoön's warnings are hurriedly dismissed when he is suddenly set upon and killed by monstrous sea serpents, seemingly sent by divine command to punish his sacrilegious response to the horse, while in other literary and visual inflections of the myth, the trick with the horse is devised by Athena herself.[8] For ancient audiences, the Trojan Horse was not only a mortal ruse, but a divine deceit.

More than a plot twist in an ancient story, the Trojan Horse vividly indexes something of the sociocultural anxieties bound up with the bestowing and receiving of gifts. Enmeshed within a wider web of social relationships, cultural preferences and economies of exchange, gifts are freighted with meanings and values extending beyond the gift itself: as an invested social act, gift-giving is entangled not only with culturally specific constructs of reciprocity and obligation, but with uncertainty, unpredictability, and the risk of triggering offence or rejection.[9] In the

1.1 Dated to the second century CE, this beautifully wrought intaglio stamp seal only a few centimetres wide shows the mysterious wooden horse dwarfing Troy's city gate. The doomed citadel can be seen in the background. Oxford, Ashmolean Museum, AN1892.1576.

ancient world, the complex dynamics of gift-giving were particularly pronounced in the generation, celebration and mobilization of social relationships between humans and deities. Ritually expressed as vows, offerings and sacrifices, worshippers' gifts to the gods simultaneously reflected and requested divine gifts of patronage, protection and blessings.[10] But divine–human relationships were inevitably asymmetric in social potency, rendering a neglected, offended or angered deity a dangerous reality in the religious lives of ancient peoples: divine gifts might easily be withheld, or morph into abandonment, malevolence or curses.

It is a risk revealed in an ancient tale from the southern Levant, likely composed in or around Jerusalem in the fifth century BCE, but drawing on older traditions. In the very distant past, so the story goes, two brothers gave gifts to the god Yahweh. One, an earth-tiller, offered up some fruit of the ground. The other, a shepherd, sacrificed the firstlings of his flock. Yahweh looked with favour on the shepherd, but frowned upon his brother. Angered by divine rejection, the earth-tiller turned killer: he rose up against his brother, and murdered him. In punishment, the deity expelled the earth-tiller from his presence, cursing him to scratch a living from unyielding soil at the edges of the world. Told in Genesis 4.1–16, the biblical story of Cain and Abel has long been read as a morality tale, warning against the dangerous human proclivity to jealousy, rivalry and violence (figure 1.2). But at the heart of this ancient story is the risk inherent in offering a deity the wrong sort of gift, as a closer reading of the text reveals. Yahweh appears to reject Cain's gift not because he prefers animal sacrifice to grain offerings, but because Cain is not said to offer the 'first fruits' of his harvest – the high-status, distinctively sacred portion conventionally given to ancient Levantine deities in grateful acknowledgement of the gift of agricultural fecundity. By contrast, Abel offers the cream of his crop, pointedly described in verse 4 as both 'the firstlings of his flock' and 'their fatty parts' – those succulent pieces giving off an enticing aroma when burned on an altar, and particularly favoured by God elsewhere in the Hebrew Bible (Old Testament).[11] As the story of Cain and Abel suggests, the wrong gift was not only a ritual faux pas, but a manifestation of disorder: it could rupture the social bond between a worshipper and a deity, and trigger further social deviancy and disaster in the wider community.

One of the earliest portrayals of the ordered, cosmic context of gift-giving is a narrative crafted not in words, but in images. Standing just over a metre high, the Uruk Vase was itself a gift dedicated to the Sumerian goddess

1.2 God watches from heaven as Cain kills Abel, in a late fifteenth-century CE manuscript. In the biblical story, the world's first murder is triggered by the divine rejection of Cain's offering. The Middle English text here is a prayer addressed to Abel, calling for his help to be patient in the face of human hostility. Oxford, Bodleian Library, MS. e Mus. 160, fol. 2r.

caym　abell

Abell the Juste Adam secundsson
Gudman & in lyfe Innocent
and in thy deth right pacient some
for the first martyre is then bent
thyn offeringe to god was right plecent
wherfor thy brother bayme the flower
Now pray for vs to be pacient
when that oure enmyse vs present

right

Inanna in about 3100 BCE (figure 1.3). Excavated from a deposit of cult objects in Eanna, the goddess's sacred precinct in the Mesopotamian city of Uruk, this striking alabaster vessel presents an idealized portrait of the ways in which agricultural fertility, ritual offerings and divine–human sociality structured the productive workings of a hierarchical cosmos – from its watery foundations and earthly inhabitants to its divine curators. Circling the vase's lowest register are fertile waters, from which neat, cultivated rows of barley spring; above them, male and female sheep and goats file in orderly fashion around the vase. In the middle register, the fruits of agricultural plenty are borne aloft in baskets and jugs by male priests in a ritual procession. Their destination is shown on the top register, where an elite female (either Inanna or her human representative) stands in the goddess's temple, surrounded by goats and jugs, baskets laden with food, and large vessels not unlike the Uruk Vase itself.[12] On this remarkable object, the goddess's blessings of agricultural fecundity and human prosperity are both reflected and requested in the form of ritual offerings.

The gift of writing

It was in the late fourth millennium BCE, shortly before the Uruk Vase was crafted, that the earliest written records emerged in Uruk and other early Mesopotamian cities, where sacred precincts and temples already served as economic hubs. A product of urbanism and its institutionalized, hierarchical forms of social organization and administration, early writing began as an accounting technique, whereby the movement of goods, services and labour in and out of sacred precincts was tracked using small clay tokens onto which signs and symbols representing ideas, numbers, places and things were inscribed and combined to form a 'pictographic' account.[13] Known now as 'proto-cuneiform', this method of account-keeping would give rise to cuneiform ('wedge-shaped'), the world's first full-blown writing system. And in its wake, myths about the divine gift of writing would emerge.

One such myth is the story *Inanna and Enki*, a Sumerian text dated to about 2000 BCE, but often thought to draw on older traditions about Uruk's rise or return to politico-cultural supremacy in the region.[14] The myth reflects the notion that writing was a fundamental quality or essence (called 'ME' in Sumerian) of civilized life, along with over ninety others, ranging from leatherwork, beer brewing, weaponry and lovemaking, to decision-making, heroism, priesthood and prostitution. Originating in the divine sphere, the MEs were in the custodial care of the clever god Enki, who had them stored in the Abzu, his underwater temple in the primordial city of Eridu. Eager to bestow these civilized qualities on her beloved city of Uruk, the goddess Inanna journeys to Eridu, where she coaxes Enki into a drinking competition, and tricks the drunken god into ritually gifting her the MEs: 'In the name of my power, in the name of my Abzu, I will give to holy Inanna', Enki repeatedly vows, as each tranche of MEs is given over to the goddess.[15] Loading them onto a boat, Inanna travels back to Uruk, overcoming various attempts by a now sober Enki to regain the MEs. Docking at the city, Inanna unloads her cargo, and the people of Uruk are able to write.

Certain features of this myth bear closer consideration, for the story throws into sharp relief the ambiguous nature of gift-giving. Inanna willingly gives the MEs to Uruk, but this is not a disinterested act. The myth's inventory of civilized essences is weighted towards those activities particularly associated with Inanna's cult.[16] Bestowing these gifts not only enhances the goddess's prestige by enculturating her favourite city, but facilitates and enriches the performance of rituals binding humans into a social relationship with her. The myth also reminds us that even those gifts which appear to be freely given can instead be coaxed, cajoled or manipulated from their donors, just as Enki discovers. Modern readers might assume that Inanna's duplicity is antisocial behaviour, at odds with the idealized, civilizing MEs here understood to structure divine and human communities. But in this story, deceit is included among the MEs procured from Enki – himself the ultimate trickster god – and it was a skill closely associated with the canny heroism often exhibited by deities and their favoured mortals across the ancient world – much as Homer's portrayals of 'crafty' Odysseus in the *Odyssey* and *Iliad* illustrate.[17] Accordingly, in another Sumerian text enjoying a long afterlife in Mesopotamian cultures, it is by means of duplicity and deceit that the legendary Gilgamesh captures and defeats the monstrous Huwawa (also known as Humbaba), the divine guardian of the gods' faraway Forest of Cedars. Seeking to disarm his fearsome foe, Gilgamesh tricks Huwawa into divesting himself of his protective auras in exchange for promised gifts of kinship (via marriage to Gilgamesh's sisters), urban living (two pairs of sandals for Huwawa's paws) and luxurious goods more usually offered to

1.3 Dated to about 3100 BCE, this striking alabaster vessel was excavated from Inanna's sacred precinct in Uruk, in what is now southern Iraq. The inextricable bonds between agricultural abundance, human prosperity and offerings to the gods are presented in a coherent, visual narrative. Baghdad, Iraq Museum, IM 19606.

deities (figure 1.4). For the seemingly isolated Huwawa, they are tempting gifts, indexing sociality, civilized status and material prestige. And yet what he receives instead is a punch in the face – swiftly followed by the loss of his head in a brutal decapitation.[18]

But in returning more specifically to the divine gift of writing, the most striking feature of *Inanna and Enki* is its pointedly concrete portrayal of the gift itself. Along with the other MEs, 'the craft of the scribe' (writing) is stored in the Abzu, then stowed on a boat and offloaded at Uruk. Here, writing is as much a material object as a socializing, civilized skill. This notion is itself materialized and exemplified by the clay tablets on which ancient south-west Asian myths and traditions about the gods were typically inscribed, curated and copied by professional scribes, right into the first millennium BCE. In the elevated sociopolitical milieux in which writing and scribalism predominantly operated, it was well understood that the gods had always been in possession of inscribed objects such as these – although, in a particularly prominent stream of Mesopotamian tradition, the tablets on which deities wrote were not usually clay, but lapis lazuli. From catalogues of oracles and omens detailing the destinies of kingdoms and mortals, to the blueprints of temples that kings and rulers were instructed to build, the gods could write realities into being by crafting and inscribing their own tablets. Some of these texts might be gifted to rulers in dreams, revealed to diviners in signs and symbols, or even consulted as clay copies in temple archives and royal libraries. Indeed, according to a catalogue in King Ashurbanipal's famous library in Nineveh, Assyria (seventh century BCE), the archives held nine works composed by the god Ea (Enki) himself, while others were said to have been dictated by Ea and written by scribes.[19] As both a cultural practice and a material object, the divine gift of writing left tangible traces, simultaneously modelling and facilitating a continued social exchange between deities and humans.

The social relationship between gods and worshippers was often written into the very fabric of temples and other high-status buildings dedicated to deities. Across ancient south-west Asian cultures, temple-building and renovation were primarily a royal activity, ideologically bound to a king's complex archetypal role as the gods' chosen representative and foremost cultic servant. More than a monumental symbol of divine presence, a temple was a divine dwelling place – literally the 'house' of the god – rendering its royal builder a gift-giver in service of the resident deity. And in some societies

previous pages **1.4** Inscribed on both sides, a cuneiform clay tablet details part of the Sumerian story of *Gilgamesh and Huwawa*. The fearsome Huwawa is disempowered when Gilgamesh tricks him into stripping off his divine auras in exchange for promised gifts. Oxford, Ashmolean Museum, AN1932.0155. Kish (modern Tell Uhaimir), Iraq, *c.* 1900 – 1600 BCE.

this royal duty was materially built into a temple's brickwork or foundations in the form of ritually empowered dedicatory inscriptions. Positioned at conceptually and structurally meaningful places (beneath thresholds, or on doorways, or at corners), these inscriptions functioned both as protective amulets and as 'speaking' stones or 'broadcasting' bricks, forever reminding the deity of the king who had built their temple. Like Inanna's concrete cargo of writing, these inscriptions were at once social agents and material objects.

An early example is now housed in Oxford's Ashmolean Museum. Seemingly commissioned by the Mesopotamian king Shulgi of Ur (r. 2094–2047 BCE), it is an inscribed stone tablet, which was once interred in a brick box beneath the foundations of Bagara, the temple of the warrior-god Ningirsu, in the ancient city of Girsu, in what is now southern Iraq (figure 1.5). Comprising eight lines of Sumerian on the tablet's obverse, and two on its reverse, the inscription is formulaic in style, but illustrates well the sociality of both the tablet and the temple as a gift to the deity:

> [1–4]   For the god Ningirsu, mighty hero of the
>   god Enlil, his lord,
> [5–8]   Shulgi, mighty man, king of Ur, king of the lands
>   of Sumer and Akkad,
> [9–10]   built his temple of Bagara for him.[20]

Royal inscriptions and other specialist texts from ancient south-west Asia can often impart an alluring awe in signalling the ritual and cosmic efficacy of writing as a material 'gift' to the gods, reflecting the prestige of writing itself as an activity primarily restricted to higher-status socio-economic groups. But the extent to which inscribed foundation bricks and other temple inscriptions were similarly considered inherently powerful objects by construction-site workers and other ordinary folk, as opposed to the elites commissioning and using these buildings, is less certain. Indeed,

1.5 Ritually interred beneath the foundations of the god Ningirsu's temple in the ancient city of Girsu, this inscribed tablet essentially 'spoke' to the deity about the temple's royal builder, Shulgi of Ur. Oxford, Ashmolean Museum, AN1922.0009. Girsu (modern Telloh), Iraq, *c*. 2100–2000 BCE.

paw prints (and occasionally human footprints) on some bricks made for temples and high-status buildings indicate that when the wet bricks were left out to dry, they were not necessarily deemed 'special' enough to be guarded from roaming feet – not even if they bore royal inscriptions invoking the gods, as some examples from Mesopotamia and neighbouring regions suggest.[21] It is a reminder, perhaps, that while gifts can play a performative role in the wider community in promoting the relationship between the donor and the recipient, the social power of the gift ultimately pivots around the particular relationship that the gift itself constitutes – at times one between powerful gods and earthly elites.

Gifting identity and embodiment

It is against this broader cultural backdrop of gifts and writing that biblical constructs of 'sacred' texts can be better understood. Although there is some evidence to suggest that the scriptures of ancient Judaism and early Christianity (which began as a minor Jewish cult) might occasionally end up in a rubbish dump (figure 1.6), the scribal curators of these authoritative texts had long imbued them with a 'holiness' signalling their status as both divine revelation and sacred ritual objects.[22] It was a status drawing in part on older, ancient Israelite ideas about the paradigmatic sociality and materiality of divine *torah* – a biblical Hebrew term which properly means 'teaching' or 'instruction', but which also serves as a shorthand label for the 'law' Yahweh is said to have given to Moses on Mount Sinai. By the closing centuries of the first millennium BCE, the label 'Torah' had also come to designate the most authoritative collection of religious writings circulating among Yahweh-worshipping communities across ancient south-west Asia and the eastern Mediterranean: the books (or scrolls) of Genesis, Exodus, Leviticus, Numbers and Deuteronomy were now identified as the very law (Torah) Yahweh had gifted to Moses to transmit to the Israelites. And it is the ancient tradition about this divine gift that has given these scriptures their sacred status.

Compiled in about the fifth century BCE, the story is told in a series of convoluted narratives across Exodus, and repeated – with some notable variations – in Deuteronomy, rendering the precise nature of the gift itself difficult to discern: it is confusingly depicted as both a pair of stone tablets, on which Yahweh inscribes front and back with his very finger the Ten Commandments, and as a lengthy divine speech, subsequently recorded

1.6 A second- or third-century CE fragment of the Septuagint, the Greek translation of the Hebrew scriptures, excavated from an ancient rubbish dump in Oxyrhynchus, Egypt. The text is Genesis 24.31–42, in which Abraham's servant procures Rebekah as a wife for Isaac in exchange for gifts. Oxford, Bodleian Library, MS. Gr. bib. d. 5 (P) (P. Oxy. 656).

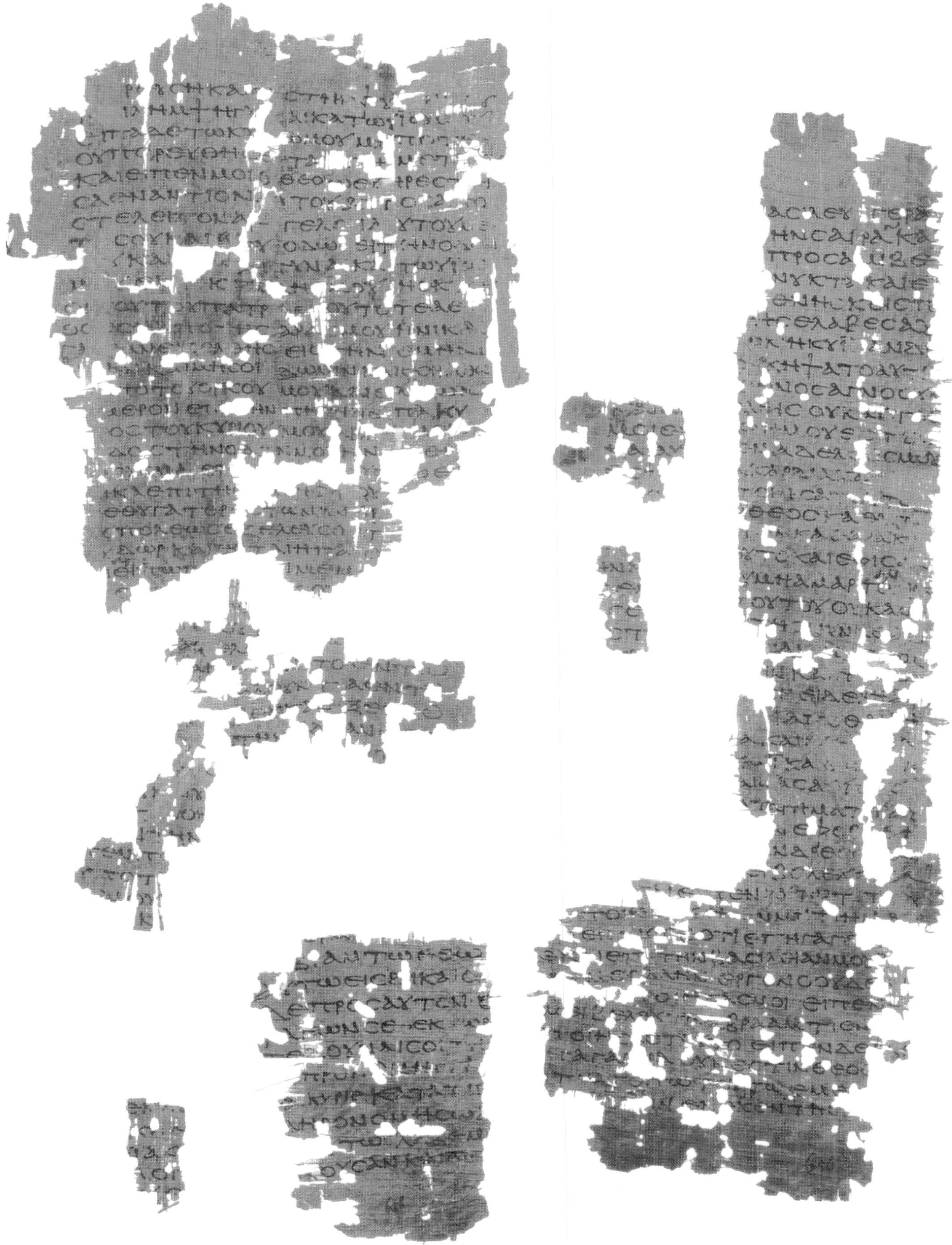

in a scroll by Moses (in some texts known as 'the book of the covenant'). Both forms of the gift are nonetheless rendered concretely iconic in materializing the binding social relationship between God and the Israelites. This relationship is covenantal in nature: like a treaty, it binds parties together, forcefully casting 'Torah' as a gift constituting the special social relationship between God and the Israelites.

But the giving of the Torah is more than a tale of gift-giving in the very distant past, as a remarkable image in a late thirteenth-century Jewish manuscript indicates. Crafted in southern Germany, the Laud Mahzor is an Ashkenazic book of festival prayers, rich in colourful miniatures, many of which offer visual commentaries on these festal liturgies. And at the top of the page opening the feast of Shavuot – also known as the Festival of the Giving of the Torah – we can see the Torah descending from the heavens (figure 1.7). Reflecting the Hebrew Bible's blurred distinctions between the tablets of the Ten Commandments and the written Torah, God's covenantal gift is seen in double vision: although a winged divine emissary presents two stone tablets to the assembled Israelites, their outstretched hands receive the Torah scroll. In keeping with the aniconic tendencies of Judaism, the faces of all the figures in this particular scene are distorted. The Israelites are equipped with bird-like facial features (perhaps better understood as higher-status griffin heads), while the face of the divine being is almost entirely blank.[23] God himself is instead 'represented' in the centre of the page, for the hymn's opening word, *adon* ('Lord'), is enlarged and enshrined in a temple-like space. Within this space, the blood of a sacrificial animal is sprinkled on God's people in an altar scene usually understood to show Moses ritually solemnizing the covenant relationship in Exodus 24.8: 'Moses took the blood and dashed it on the people, and said, "See the blood of the covenant that the LORD has made with you in accordance with all these words [in the scroll of the covenant]."'[24] As the juxtaposition of images and text on this page of the Laud Mahzor suggests, those reciting this hymn at the beginning of Shavuot were not simply commemorating God's gift of the Torah to their biblical ancestors; they were celebrating the continued material presence of this ancient gift in their own religious lives. The divinely crafted covenant that had been written in stone was the Torah scroll – the same Torah scroll that was read aloud in their synagogues, where 'all these words' of the covenant could be seen and heard.

1.7 God's gift of the Torah descends from the heavens in a magnificent late-thirteenth-century Jewish prayer book from southern Germany, now known as the Laud Mahzor. The divinely crafted stone tablets (top left) are identified with the Torah scroll used in worship (top right). Oxford, Bodleian Library, MS. Laud Or. 321, fol. 127v.

אָמְנֵנוּ
אֻנְזְלוּ שְׁכְנֵנוּ
אֲרָם הִקְצֵנוּ
יֵין קַנֵּנוּ
בְּנֵין בְּעָרֵטוּ
כִּי שֵׁץ יְרֵטוּ
בְּשֶׁעְטוּעֵי בְּרֵטוּ
רֹאשֵׁיה הֲרֵטוּ

But the written words of the Torah could also be embodied. From as early as the second century BCE some Jewish groups were wearing *tefillin* (phylacteries) – small pouches or boxes containing tiny scrolls bearing holy words from the Torah.[25] Fixed to the head and arm with long leather straps, they are still worn in prayer by some Jewish men (and, increasingly, some women) today (figure 1.8). These ritual objects manifest obedience to one of the most authoritative instructions in the Torah – an instruction which is itself inscribed upon one of the tiny scrolls housed within the *tefillin* boxes:

1.8 Used in prayer, *tefillin* (phylacteries) bind tiny scrolls containing parts of the Torah to the worshipper's body (*opposite page*). These eighteenth-century CE examples accompany an Ashkenazi Torah scroll (*right*). Oxford, Christ Church MS 201a (central European, possibly Czech).

Keep these words that I am commanding you today in your heart. Recite them to your children and speak them when you are in your house and when you are walking on the road, when you lie down and when you rise. Bind them as a sign on your hand, fix them as an emblem between your eyes. Write them on the doorposts of your house and on your gates.

(Deuteronomy 6.6–9)

In this biblical text the Torah is a potent form of body modification. It is fixed onto the body as an amulet, and recalled, incanted and displayed. Its performative function is further embodied in its recitation when rising, walking, resting and lying down. And written into the community's doorways like a protective ritual inscription it modifies the social body, too.[26] In giving the Torah, God was understood to have given shape to the bodily and communal identities of his worshippers across the generations.

From the Trojan Horse to the giving of the Torah, ancient myths about gods and gifts resonate into the present day. But unlike Athena – or Inanna and Enki – it is the God of the Bible who has managed to maintain a foothold in the religious landscapes of the modern world. It is a distant reflection, perhaps, of that pervasive notion in the biblical imagination that the granting of the Torah was the gift that keeps on giving.

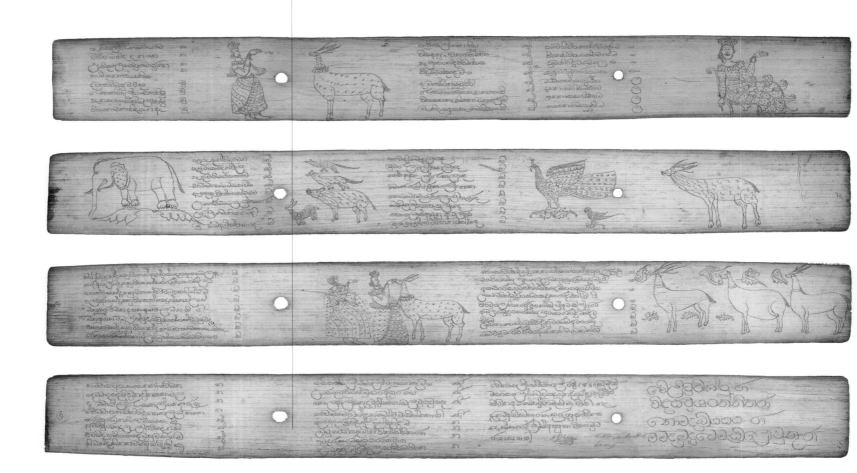

2.1 Four folios from a palm-leaf manuscript of the *Muva Jātakaya* by Agonis Peiris of Ratnapura (Sri Lanka), dated 1864 CE. This is a versified version in Sinhala language of the *Birth Story of the Deer*. Oxford, Bodleian Library, MS. Sinh. b. 27 (R).

Chapter 2

Writing the Body and Gifting the Dharma: Buddhist Traditions of Gift, Text and Knowledge

Camillo A. Formigatti

The following short tale is part of the frame story of the *Sutra of the Wise and the Foolish*, known in Tibetan as the *Mdo mdzangs blun* and in Mongolian as the *Ocean of Narratives* (Mongolian *Üliger-un-dalai*). I start with it because this story encapsulates some key concerns about the transmission of knowledge and the centrality of giving in the Buddhist tradition:

> Thus have I heard at one time: when the Victorious, Perfectly-Departed Enlightened One [the Buddha] had entered the great realm of victory and had achieved Supreme Enlightenment, he dwelt in the land of Magadha. And the thought came to him: 'Of what benefit can I be to beings of this world who have long been blinded by false views which are difficult to correct? It would be better to attain final Nirvana.'
>
> The deities of the Realm of Brahmā, perceiving the thoughts of the Blessed One, descended from their realm, prostrated themselves at his feet, folded their palms in devotion, and pleaded with him to turn the Wheel of Law…
>
> Again, Lord, Countless aeons ago, there lived in Benares five-hundred sages with their teacher, Utpala. Utpala wandered here and there in search of the Divine Law to learn and meditate upon and at one time proclaimed: 'If anyone can teach me the Divine Law, I shall become his slave.'
>
> A Brahmin teacher, hearing these words, said: 'I have the Divine Law. If you require it, I will teach it to you.'
>
> The sage bowed low before the Brahmin, pressed his palms together in reverence, and said: 'Great Teacher, have compassion on me and teach me the Law.'
>
> The Brahmin answered: 'It is exceedingly difficult to learn the Divine Law. I have learned it only by enduring

great sufferings. If you wish to learn the True Law, will you do as I command?'

When the sage answered: 'Great Teacher, command, and I shall obey,' the Brahmin said: 'Cut off your skin and make paper. Make ink of your blood, and write the Law. Then I shall teach it to you.'

With great joy and devotion the sage, in reverence for the Law of the Enlightened Ones, flayed his skin, made a pen from his bones, and mixed his blood into ink. Then he said: 'The time has come, Teacher, quickly teach me the Law and I shall write it.'

The Brahmin teacher then spoke these two verses:

> 'Control the acts of the body.
> Do not passionately desire the thief who destroys the mind.
> Do not speak false, harsh, or thoughtless words.
> Do not abandon yourself to desire.
> Cut off thoughts of anger.
> When all wrong views are cut off …
> This is the Supreme.
> This is the course of the bodhisattvas.'

When the sage had written these verses, he was glorified throughout all Jambudvīpa and men endeavored with great zeal to learn what he had taught and to cut off evil deeds. It was you, Lord, who at that time, with no thoughts of regret, underwent great suffering to find the Law for the sake of many beings.[27]

The *Sutra of the Wise and the Foolish* from which this extract comes is a collection of tales of the previous lives of the Buddha Śākyamuni and of *bodhisattva*s (those on the path to buddhahood), and is transmitted in both the Chinese and Tibetan Buddhist canons. A Chinese pilgrim translated it in the Uyghur kingdom of Qocho around 445 from central Asian sources transmitted orally. Later, the Chinese version, called *Xian yu jing*, was translated into the Tibetan language.[28] Albeit gruesome in parts, this story helps to explain the importance of knowledge and gift-giving in

Buddhism, since it contains many elements central to both: the importance of spreading the Dharma – the doctrine of the Buddha, translated here as 'the (True) Law'; the role of writing in its transmission; and the supreme act of giving in the form of self-sacrifice.

The perfection of giving and the sacrificial body

In the Buddhist tradition, stories about the previous lives of the Buddha similar to this one from the *Sutra of the Wise and the Foolish* are called *jātaka* and *avadāna* in Sanskrit.[29] The narrative material making up these stories is already found in bas-reliefs and sculptures of Buddhist religious monuments such as the *stūpa*s of Bharhut and Sanchi (both in central India), dating back to the end of the second and the beginning of the first centuries BCE.[30] Later literary versions of *jātaka*s and *avadāna*s have come down to us in many works written in the different languages of Buddhism. Although they may differ considerably in style and genre, they always use a threefold structure, consisting of a story of the present (Sanskrit *pratyutpannavastu*, set at the time of the narrator, usually the Buddha or a Buddhist saint); a story of the past (Sanskrit *atītavastu*); and finally the identification of the characters in the present with those in the past – that is, in their former births (Sanskrit *samavadhāna*). The passage above from the *Sutra of the Wise and the Foolish* also begins with the story of the present, in which the deities of the Realm of Brahmā try to dissuade the Buddha from his purpose of attaining final Nirvana. They tell him that the time has come to turn the Wheel of the Dharma to help all living beings attain liberation from *saṃsāra*, the ocean of rebirth and suffering. In order to convince him, they recount to the Buddha several occasions in his previous lives in which he sacrificed even his own body for the sake of spreading the Dharma, including the story of Utpala. Each of these stories of the past is followed by the identification between past and present. The deities manage to persuade the Buddha to set the Wheel of the Dharma in motion in the Deer Park in Varanasi; he then starts teaching the Dharma to all living beings, including deities and mythical creatures such as *nāga*s (serpents), *yakṣa*s (nature spirits) and *asura*s (demigods).

The 'course of the bodhisattvas' at the end of Utpala's story is the spiritual path followed by a living being who wants to generate *bodhicitta* ('aspiration to enlightenment'), in order to achieve buddhahood. The so-called bodhisattva path stretches over a huge number of lifetimes during which the bodhisattva proceeds through a series of stages, developing a set of specific virtues known in Sanskrit as *pāramitā*s, usually rendered as 'perfections'. One of these is the perfection of giving (Sanskrit *dāna*). Others include morality (Sanskrit *śīla*), patience or forbearance (Sanskrit *kṣānti*), effort (Sanskrit *vīrya*), concentration (Sanskrit *dhyāna*) and wisdom (Sanskrit *prajñā*). These six perfections are the subject of the *Compendium of the Perfections* (Sanskrit *Pāramitāsamāsa*), a work attributed to the renowned author Āryaśūra, probably active in the beginning of the fifth century CE, perhaps even earlier.[31] Āryaśūra's poetic masterpiece *Garland of the Buddha's Past Lives* (Sanskrit *Jātakamālā*) seems to use the first three perfections to structure its first thirty stories. Its very first narrative, the *Birth Story on the Tigress* (Sanskrit *Vyāghrījātaka*) is a version of the story that also follows the frame tale of Utpala in the *Sutra of the Wise and the Foolish*. It recounts how Prince Mahāsattva gives away his own body to a hungry tigress in order to avoid her eating her own cubs, an act of sacrifice that distils the meaning of the Perfection of Giving.

Such moments of bodily sacrifice recur in a number of Buddhist narratives. Another very famous *jātaka* in which the bodhisattva sacrifices himself to save other beings from suffering and death is narrated in the drama *Joy of the Nāgas* (Sanskrit *Nāgānanda*), composed by King Harṣa at the beginning of the seventh century CE. Here, in a previous life the bodhisattva was Jimūtavāhana, 'a prince of the divine magicians (*vidyādhara*s), who substitutes himself for a serpent (*nāga*) who has been designated as the tithe given by the snake community for consumption that day by Garuḍa, the king of the birds'.[32] The *Birth Story of the Deer* (Pāli *Nigrodhamigajātaka*), found in the Pāli canon, shares the same motifs and structure of the *Joy of the Nāgas* (figures 2.1 and 2.2). This *jātaka* narrates how the chief of the deer agrees to present to the king on a regular basis one doe for his consumption, in order to avoid other deer suffering from random royal hunts, and the bodhisattva then substitutes himself for the doe whose turn it is.[33] Stories exemplifying the Perfection of Giving are very popular in all Buddhist traditions, and the story of Prince Viśvantara (Pāli *Vessantara*) is probably the most famous and celebrated of all, particularly in South East Asia (figure 2.3). In this story, Viśvantara performs several acts of generosity. When the population of the neighbouring kingdom is suffering because of a terrible drought, he gives away the magic elephant that ensures adequate rainfall to his country, forcing his father King Sañjaya

2.2 A detail from figure 2.1. Here the king touches the nose of the deer-king, while behind him the queen raises her hands for an offering. Oxford, Bodleian Library, MS. Sinh. b. 27 (R), fol. 12v.

៕ ។ ៕ ឃេយងេសិរួ៧ៗៗ

។ ៕ នេសរួបេ៧ៗៗៗ៧ៗៗ

៕ នេសរាបិ៧ៗៗៗៗៗ

ណិៗៗៗ ៗ ៗ ណ៧ហ្ម៧៧៧

បិ៧ៗៗៗៗៗ ណៗ

ៗៗៗៗៗៗៗ ៗ ៗ ណៗៗៗ

ៗៗៗៗៗៗ ណៗៗៗៗ

ៗៗ ៕ នេសរាបិៗ

៕ នេសរួបេ៧ៗៗៗៗ

ៗៗៗ ៕ ឃេយៗ

2.3 The story of Prince Viśvantara's generosity. An eighteenth-century Thai *samut khoi* (mulberry paper manuscript), lavishly illuminated and containing several different texts in Pāli. On this folio, the two miniatures depict Viśvantara giving away his wife to the god Śakra disguised as a Brahmin, and his children to the Brahmin Jūjaka. Oxford, Bodleian Library, MS. Pali a. 27 (R), fol. 17.

to banish him. Viśvantara then renounces all his possessions and with his family settles down in a remote grove in a forest. One day while his wife is away, he gives away his children to a Brahmin who wants to enslave them, and when he is about to give away his wife as well, Śakra, the king of the gods, intervenes and prevents him from doing it. These extreme stories of giving help to explain the finest points of the Buddhist doctrine, at the same time using the theme of giving as a way to embed their salvific purpose in the minds of the audience.

Gift-books and bodies of knowledge

The story of Utpala from the *Sutra of the Wise and the Foolish* with which we began not only illustrates the centrality of giving in Buddhism, but is also an excellent example of the importance of writing technology in spreading the word of the Buddha. It introduces the concept of the donation of books in Buddhism as pious gifts to acquire merit in the next life for oneself, and for all living beings. This aspect of book production is mentioned explicitly in a formula occurring quite often in colophons (inscriptions or notes) that appear in Buddhist Sanskrit manuscripts containing various texts:

> What[ever] religious merit is [contained] here [in this book], it should arise [from this donation]; keeping in the foreground the *ācārya*s, the *upādhyāya*s and the parents, the reward of supreme insight is attained for the sake of all categories of beings.[34]

This formula occurs in early Buddhist inscriptions and manuscript colophons. In later manuscripts it follows the mention of the donor or donors who commissioned the copying (figure 2.4). In this formulation a gift has effects not only on its recipient(s), but reaches out much more widely. In the story of Utpala, the idea of sacrificing one's own body, or at least part of it, links directly with the idea that writing down the Buddha's word is particularly meritorious: the bodhisattva uses his own skin as writing material, his own bones as writing implement, and his own blood as ink! As in medieval Christianity with its veneration for the Bible as a holy object, and Christ as the Word made flesh, the cult of the book in Buddhism is akin in importance to the cult of relics of the Buddha's body (figure 2.5). This equation is most evident in the term *dharmaśarīra*, 'relics/

body of the dharma', which refers to the Buddha's scriptures, verses and doctrines (Sanskrit *dharma*) considered to be equal to the relics of his body (Sanskrit *śarīra*). Accordingly, small pieces of paper with mantras written or printed on them, and even whole books, were hidden in *stūpa*s (shrines) and venerated in a similar way to relics of the body of the historical Buddha, Siddhārtha Gautama. The importance of reproducing the word of the Buddha was also one of the driving motivations for the early diffusion of print technology in central Asia. The oldest dated printed book is a copy of the *Diamond Sūtra* in Chinese, produced on 11 May 868 and found in the so-called Mogao Caves or the 'Caves of a Thousand Buddhas', near Dunhuang, an oasis town on the Silk Roads (now in Gansu province, Northwest China). An even clearer example of the role of print in reproducing and spreading the word of the Buddha is the Japanese *Hyakumantō darani* prints, 'One Million Pagodas and Dharani Prayers', commissioned by the Empress Shotoku between 764 and 770 CE. These are magical formulae (Sanskrit *dhāraṇī*) in Sanskrit, written in Chinese characters and printed with woodblocks on small paper sheets. The sheets were then rolled up and housed in wooden cases resembling miniature *stūpa*s or pagodas, and are considered among the first – if not the first ever – printed texts.

Since the early stages of Buddhism, then, the central concepts of gift, sacrifice and exchange have been developed and disseminated through artful storytelling. Many of these tales belong to the broader South Asian narrative tradition, but have been reimagined in a Buddhist frame over many centuries in all Buddhist countries across Asia. Buddhist narrative literature helped structure patterns of behaviour and aspirations to perfection in both monastic and lay communities. Interwoven with all this, the donation of books themselves as a meritorious act elevates the Buddha's word, transmitted in writing, to a special kind of bodily gift.

2.4 These illuminated covers are from one of the very few surviving manuscripts of the *Perfection of Wisdom in Eight Thousand Metrical Units* copied in the eleventh century CE at the monastery of Nalandā (north-east India). A colophon (note) at the end of the manuscript contains the formula for gaining merit by copying the text. Although the name of the donor was changed at a later date, we can still tell that a female lay donor (Sanskrit *upāsikā*) originally commissioned the manuscript. Oxford, Bodleian Library, MS. Sansk. a. 7 (R).

2.5 A manuscript of the *Recitation of the Names of Mañjuśrī* (Sanskrit *Mañjuśrīnāmasangīti*), a popular liturgical work. A wonderful example of Nepalese book craft, this luxury manuscript is written on blue-black paper with golden letters, protected by two decorated wooden covers and held together by an ornate metal pin, with a lotus-shaped head embellished with hard stones. According to the colophon, the Buddhist monk Mayalasiṃhacandra commissioned the copying of this manuscript in 1570 CE, during the reign of King Mahendramalla (*c.* 1560–74). Oxford, Bodleian Library, MS. Sansk. d. 346 (R), fols 1v and 2r.

The Story of the kyls of tolous

PRENES ENGRE

MD RIA

Chapter 3

Donation and Desire in Medieval Books

Nicholas Perkins

One of the most inviting beginnings to a manuscript in the Bodleian's extraordinary medieval collections contains a picture of a man giving a book to a woman (figure 3.1). It is not spectacular in size, dripping with gold leaf or composed by a famous poet. Copied during the reign of Henry VIII and taking some design features from early printed books, it is also at the outer edge of the 'medieval'. It nevertheless helps us to see what was at stake in the countless acts of giving, receiving and reciprocating that run throughout medieval culture in Britain and beyond.

The main text in this book, MS. Ashmole 45, is *The Erle of Tolous*, a romance whose title is written with an elaborate strapwork letter 'T' in a style characteristic of London documents of the late 1520s. The scribe has signed his name 'Morganus' in tiny writing within an initial letter on the next page. But the centre of the page is taken up with the Flemish-style illustration, sealing this book as a gift. The young man holds his hat in one hand, and with the other he passes a book (holding Ashmole 45, you feel that it's *this* book) to the young woman, whose hands are open to receive it, though in the picture will never quite do so. At this time, speech was often represented in a scroll; here it says 'Prenes engre' *(Take with pleasure)*. They look like a well-to-do couple, perhaps engaged to be married, with the book as a gift that helps cement that relationship. Underneath the couple, the words 'Maid Maria' are cleverly worked into two monograms, probably naming Ashmole 45's recipient.[35]

The Erle of Tolous contains mixed messages about gifts, service and family values. It's a poem of love, loyalty and justice in which the eponymous Earl falls in love with Beulybon, the wife of an emperor who is also his enemy, and later (disguised as a monk) saves her from false accusations of adultery. This earns the thanks of the emperor, who conveniently dies soon after, leaving the Earl and Beulybon to marry.

3.1 This presentation scene marks a moment of gift-giving in 1520s London. 'Maid Maria', written in two monograms underneath the young couple, is probably the name of its first recipient. Oxford, Bodleian Library, MS. Ashmole 45, fol. 2r.

When they first meet, the Earl is also in disguise, as a poor hermit, and Beulybon tellingly slips a ring amongst the coins she gives him. Finding it later, the Earl exclaims,

> My dere derlyng
> On thi finger this was;
> Wele is me I have that grace, *I am happy to have that fortune*
> Of thee to have this ryng …
> This may be owre tokenyng.[36]   *our [love] token*

The ring as 'tokenyng' signals the relationship's potential. More than this, it makes a promise to the audience about the story's conclusion, encircling the main protagonists in its narrative scope. We too will return to lovers and rings later.

At one level, Ashmole 45's presentation picture simply reminds us about the pleasures of giving and receiving books, and the romance shows how generosity returns in unpredictable ways, while meanness withers both relationships and narratives. But we might also ask how the Ashmole 45 couple fit into a network of gifts, counter-gifts and obligations. This larger network is what Marcel Mauss influentially described as a 'système des prestations totales', or system of overall obligations.[37] Did a wealthy parent pay for the book or the illustration? Was this a relationship as much between families and their desires, as between young lovers? Aspects of gender and hierarchy in gift-giving have also come under much scrutiny.[38] What did Maria really think of this gift, and its imperative to receive with pleasure? She is not given an answering voice here. Across and beyond this period, women have often been treated as an economic asset to be exchanged through marriage, even when those deals are cloaked in the language of romance. Ashmole 45 allows us to glimpse such complex negotiations of status, motivation and desire, reminding us that gifts are acts, and they prompt other acts, whether receiving or refusing, consuming, passing on or reciprocating. Gift dynamics are everywhere in medieval culture, but in this chapter I shall focus on land and power; on romantic desire; and on religion and ethics. The gifts on offer will include books, rings and horns, advice, bribes and, courtesy of Geoffrey Chaucer, an eloquent fart.

3.2 A diploma (royal charter) records a grant of land by King Æthelred. It is witnessed by religious and secular leaders as a lasting record of the gift. Oxford, Bodleian Library, MS. Eng. hist. a. 2 (item VI) (England, 998).

In nomine summi cæli qui quadrifida mundi moderamina moderando gubernat nobis ergo karissimi in Christo

illius ergo prædicatoris sententia diligenter consideranda est si nihil intulimus in hunc mundum uerum nec auferre quid possumus sed sicut illa generalis mater de qua dictum terræ es et in terram ibis nos nudos ueraciter procreauit sicut eam nos nudos excipere debet nisi aliquis diuino instinctu amore adhuc idoneus sit ut adeptus res pro omnipotentia deo expiatione peccaminum suorum pauperibus ædificiis beniuola mente distribuere uoluerit cælum thesaurum thesaurizare makat cælorum culminibus. Hinc ego ÆÐELRED altithrono amminiculante anglorum ceterarumque gentium in circuitu nationum præsidens basileus aliquam terræ particulam addo donandum cuidam leofrino meo fidelissimo duce id est uii tributariorum ædium non tamen in uno loco sed maioribus uillulis in Sihtham iii mansas et Hlodbroces hrodbury namque iiii mansas et cætera inter illos diuisum una cum manentibus cum pratis cum omnibus bonis ad illam terram pertinentibus in perpetuam hereditatem et quamdiu lux fulgebit super terram et hanc donationem dabo cum omni libertate nisi arce et pontis instructione et expeditione et ab hominibus aliis nouo signo aut qua causis perpetualiter in libertatem compono siquis uero tam epylempticus phtisi argia seductus amentia quod non optamus hanc nostræ munificentiæ dapsilitatem ausu temerario infringere temptauerit sit ipse alienatus a consortio sanctæ dei ecclesiæ necnon et a participatione sacro sancto corporis et sanguinis ihesu christi filii dei per quem totus terrarum orbis ab antiquo humani generis inimico liberatus est et cum iuda christi proditore sinistra in parte deputatus nisi prius hic digna satisfactione sua deo humiliter pænituerit.

þis synt þa gemæro · to þære hide at Lange mere to Sihtham · iii hide to Bunnan · þonne forþ to porlata · þã ponn...

[Old English boundary clause continues]

manforde.

Hæc cartula karaxata est anno dominicæ incarnationis dcccLxxxxviii huius munificentiæ singrapha infra scriptorum consentibus quorum inferius nomina secundum uniuscuiusque dignitatem caraxantur. agie crucis roborantur.

+ Ego Æðelred Britanniæ rex anglorum monarchus pro formatis appropinquare uidetur ego donationem hoc a me

+ Ego Ælfric dorobernensis ecclesiæ archiepiscopus eiusdem regis beniuolentia subscripsi.

+ Ego Aldulf eboracensis basilicæ primas hoc eulogium agie crucis taumate confirmaui.

+ Ego Ælfheah wentaneldensis cœnobii antistes subeunte rege tropheum sanctæ crucis impressi.

+ Ego Ælfheah wintoniensis ecclesiæ præsul canonica subscriptione hoc donum corroboraui.

+ Ego Wulfstan episcopus lundoniensis studium sanctæ crucis hanc regali dapsilitate libens adposui.

+ Ego Wulfsige scireburnensis ecclesiæ catascopus donum eiusdem regis confirmaui.

+ Ego Aþulf herefordensis ecclesiæ pontifex consensum præbui.

+ Ego Æþelwold episcopus hoc eulogium annui propria apicibus depinxi.

+ Ego Ælfsige	abb.	+ Ego Æðelweard	dux.	+ Ego Ordulf	m̄
+ Ego Ælfweard	abb.	+ Ego Ælfric	dux.	+ Ego Æðelmær	m̄
+ Ego Wulfgar	abb.	+ Ego Ælfhelm	dux.	+ Ego Wulfheah	m̄
+ Ego Leofric	abb.	+ Ego Leofwine	dux.	+ Ego Wulfgeat	m̄

'I hereby grant …'

One important use of written documents in pre-Conquest Britain was to record the granting of land, often from lord to retainer. The gift could be made by a formal speech act accompanied by a symbolic gesture or object, but a charter recorded that moment, recreating the gift act and becoming lasting proof of it. A diploma (royal charter) issued in 998 by King Æthelred (r. 978–1013; 1014–1016), grants land to a high-ranking man named Leofwine (figure 3.2). It uses the elevated language of a formal gift, starting with the Chi Rho symbol (invoking Christ), and praising God, source of all wealth. God also enables the king to sit atop the earthly hierarchy: 'ego Æþelred, altithrono amminiculante Anglorum ceterarumque gentium in circuitu triuiatim persistentium basileus' (*I Æthelred, with the support of the one enthroned on high, king of the English and of other peoples around far and wide*), using the elaborate Greek borrowing *basileus* for king. Æthelred's generosity and power are underlined by the rhetorical permanence of this gift: it is to last 'quamdiu lux fulgebit super terram' (*while light radiates over the earth*). We also learn that the previous incumbent of some of the land, Wistan, forfeited it because of 'unrihtum monslihte' (*unlawful killing*). The grant's boundaries (around Ladbroke, Radbourne and Southam in modern Warwickshire) and its tenure are then described, first briefly in Latin and then in English, the script relaxing into a less formal style, and using features of the land such as streams and fords to draw a verbal map of the gift.

After a dating clause, the document is witnessed in order of seniority, starting with King Æthelred, Ælfric the Archbishop of Canterbury, and Aldulf Archbishop of York, then on through bishops, abbots and ealdormen (nobles and regional leaders). Each is given a speaking part 'ego … roboraui; ego … confirmaui' (*I have endorsed; I have confirmed*), a performance of the gift that makes them part of its ongoing and active work. The crosses signal their agreement, give the document religious as well as royal authority, and help make the charter a visual reminder of the structure of hierarchy in Æthelred's kingdom.[39]

Whatever Æthelred 'Unræd' (Noble counsel, Bad counsel: a nickname that comes down to us as 'the Unready') claimed about his gift's longevity, Viking raids had already harried his kingdom. The English had offered huge tributes (called *gafol*; later termed *danegeld*), and many tribulations were to follow before Æthelred's death in 1016. The Old English poem

3.3 The Old English poem *Genesis B* dramatizes Lucifer's pride and fall from Heaven, having betrayed the gifts and loyalty of God. The picture on this page shows him falling from heaven, and below, as Satan, bound in chains in hell. Oxford, Bodleian Library, MS. Junius 11, p. 16 (England, *c*.1000).

ealra morðra mæst · swa deð monna gehpilc þe
pið his paldend pinnan ongynneð · mid mane pið
þone mæran drihten · þa pearð se mihtiga ge
bolgen · hehsta heofones palodfend · pearp hine
of þan hean stole · hete hæfde he æt his hearran
gepunnen · hyldo hæfde his ferlorene ·
gram pearð him se goda on his mode · forþon
he sceolde grund gesecean · heardes hellepiites ·
þær þe he ann pið his drihtne palodfend · acpæð hine
þa fram his hyldo · 7 hine on helle pearp · on
þa deopan dala þær he to deofle pearð · se
feond mid his geferum eallum · feollon þa ufon
of heofnum · þurh longe spa þreo niht 7 da
gas · þa hi glas of heofnum on helle · 7 hie ealle
for sceop drihten to deoflum ·

The Battle of Maldon recounts a Viking attack at Maldon in Essex in 991, and, rather like a British wartime film about Dunkirk, filters its narrative through imagery of heroic failure and the exchange of loyalty and blood. The ealdorman Byrhtnoth derides the Viking messenger's demand that the English give tribute in return for a quiet life. Rather than handing over valuable weapons and armour to buy off the attack, Byrhtnoth instead vows that the English will use their spears and swords to fight back, giving as good as they get:

> Hi willađ eow to gafole   garas syllan,
> ættrynne ord   and ealde swurd,
> þa heregeatu   þe eow æt hilde ne deah.[40]
>
> (*They* [the English] *will give you spears as tribute,*
> *deadly point and ancestral sword –*
> *war gear that won't help you in battle.*)

The grim playfulness of Byrhtnoth's language relies on the expectation in early medieval culture that guests are greeted with gifts; that exchanges of treasure or praise cement friendships; and that reciprocal acts of generosity or of violence are embedded in the structures of society (as also explored in the epic poem *Beowulf*). Byrhtnoth pledges his loyalty to King Æthelred, but is cut down in battle, thanking God in a final prayer for the benefits he enjoyed in his life. The poet immediately contrasts this bravery with two English cowards who flee, betraying the favours that Byrhtnoth had granted them and leaving the remaining warriors to pledge that they will repay their debt of loyalty in the face of approaching death.

A comparable narrative about the gifts of a generous lord being betrayed appears in an ambitiously illustrated manuscript from this time, but here the setting is heaven and the stakes are cosmic (figure 3.3). MS. Junius 11 is one of four manuscripts that between them contain the bulk of surviving Old English poetry. In *Genesis B* the poet dwells on how conflict and sin began, blaming the ungrateful pride of Lucifer. This angel of light is given a self-obsessed monologue claiming that he is God's equal. God overhears his treason and grows angry. On this page we learn that Lucifer had 'abandoned his [God's] favour' (*hyldo hæfde his forlorene*), and later that God 'declared him then out of his favour' (*Acwæd hine þa fram his hyldo*) – that word *hyldo* (meaning grace, loyalty, favour) distilling the relationship of giving and reciprocating that bound lord and servant together.[41] God casts Lucifer into hell, turning him into Satan. In the dramatic illustration, God is secure in heaven, flanked by loyal and handsomely winged angels. His large right hand is extended, indicating his power to speak and act. In his left hand he holds a book or document. Below a starry band, Lucifer and other rebels tumble naked into hell, its entrance represented as a beast's maw. In the lower section, Satan, now bound in the fiery pit and himself tormented by demons, looks back at what he has lost. The poem later describes how Satan plots his revenge by engineering the fall from grace of humans, including Eve's fateful giving of the apple to Adam. We could imagine the illustration here as a charter in picture form: God grants territory in eternity to Satan, surrounded by his court as witnesses. His gift is, however, the opposite of a reward for loyal service, and, rather than being bounded by Warwickshire streams as in Æthelred's charter, this land is demarcated by the burning rivers of hell.

Horns, rings and hearts

Both *The Battle of Maldon* and *Genesis B* mythologize a struggle over land and rights through the lens of religious conflict, but myths of the gift were also used to tell stories of alliance or resolution. The magnificent Horn of Ulf does this (figure 3.4). It was carved from an elephant tusk in the eleventh century, probably in Italy and perhaps at Amalfi, where trade from Africa and the Islamic eastern Mediterranean flourished, influencing the style of carving at its mouth. Legend has it that this is a tenure object, given to York Minster by a Viking nobleman to enact and record a grant of land. A much later chronicle claims that Ulf filled the horn with wine and placed it on the Minster's altar, dedicating the land to God and the Church, partly to resolve a dispute between his sons. Horns like this sometimes held relics or were used as sounding horns on special occasions; they also encouraged future gifts and nourished the legends that grew up around them. A comparable example is the famous Savernake Horn, now in the British Museum, while in the Old French epic *The Song of Roland*, Roland's horn, with which he finally summons help in battle from Charlemagne (dying in the process), is later filled with gold and laid on a church altar as a memorial. While not books themselves, objects like this tell stories: they act on people's imaginations long after they are given, and provoke further myth-making.

3.4 The Horn of Ulf is made of elephant ivory, probably carved in southern Italy in the eleventh century; its decorative carvings show the influence of Islamic design. It is said to have been given to York Minster to accompany and document a grant of land. York Minster, MA/TR14.

One well-known romance tale from this period revolves around a hero himself named Horn. He is a prince with God-given assets, cast out to sea as an orphan when his lands are conquered. Horn gains a reputation for beauty and prowess at his adopted court, and the king's daughter Rigmel is desperate to meet him. She gives a heap of gifts including a gold ring, a horse, greyhounds and a fine goshawk to her father's seneschal (steward) to persuade him to take Horn to her chamber. He initially tricks her by bringing Horn's companion Haderof instead. Rigmel is furious, and eventually the real assignation is arranged. Rigmel offers Horn a ring along with her body and wealth: 'Ja vus met joe mun cors, mun aveir en present' (*Now, I make you a present of my body and my possessions*).⁴² Horn accepts the ring, but they don't consummate their relationship until much later. First, Horn is unjustly exiled again, and Rigmel has an unattractive marriage arranged for her. Hearing of her plight, Horn returns in disguise and, at her wedding feast, asks Rigmel for a drink from the ceremonial horn, into which he slips the ring. When she too drinks, she discovers the ring, realizes that Horn has returned, and the tale's cycle of gift, pledge, revenge and restitution moves towards its climax.

In *The Erle of Tolous*, *The Romance of Horn* and many other medieval narratives, love tokens such as a ring or brooch develop their own trajectory or 'biography' through a story, shadowing the human protagonists and working both as symbol and as physical sign of their connection. The love token as a gift and metaphor-made-real was common in medieval social practice and imagination. Illustrated here (figure 3.5) is a posy ring (a ring with a motto or verse). The message 'kindly take this' – an English equivalent of Ashmole 45's 'Prenes engre' – turns the ring into a little romance narrative in itself, imagining it as the lover's urgent messenger that then nestles on its recipient's finger, or close to their breast if worn round the neck. Numerous examples of heart-shaped brooches with such messages survive from this period too, and a late-medieval song preserved in a Bodleian manuscript develops these metaphors of the lover's gift and the exchange of tokens (figure 3.6):

3.5 This sixteenth-century gold posy ring was probably a gift between lovers, and is typical of such tokens from the late-medieval and early modern periods. Oxford, Ashmolean Museum, AN 2011.32.

Go hert, hurt with adversite	*heart*
And let my lady thi wondis see,	*your wounds*
And say hir this as y say the:	
Farwel my joy, and welcom peyne,	
Til y se my lady agayne.	

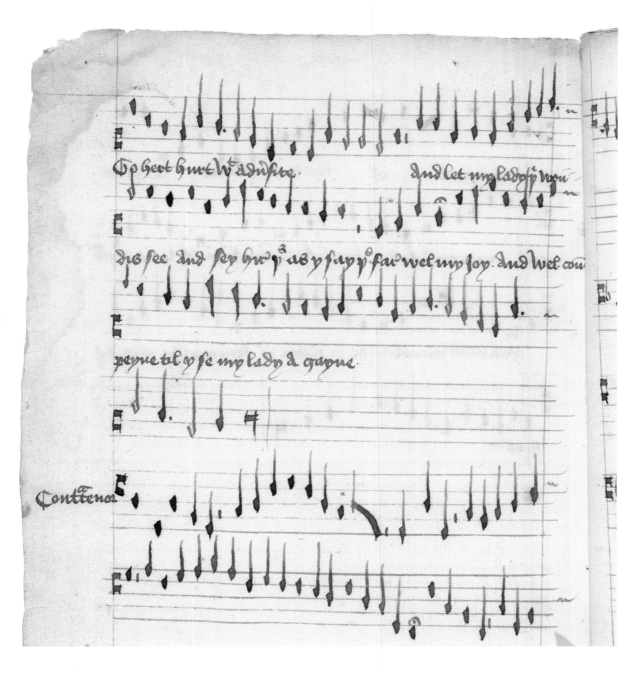

3.6 A rare survival of an English lyric with music from the fifteenth century, this song was copied with five others in a manuscript also containing an astronomical calendar. Oxford, Bodleian Library, MS. Ashmole 191, fol. 192v.

The lover sends off their heart, telling it what to declare to their beloved (and to us). The verse brings the speaker into the presence of the beloved by imagining this journey of the heart, while reminding us that 'hert' is only one letter away from 'hurt'. The heart becomes a gift of song, travelling to the lady, but also a little drama of absence and loss: 'Farwel my joy, and welcom peyne'. The lyric relies on understanding love as a gift relationship that feeds on fresh exchanges and close access to the other's body and mind.

Divine gifts, human donors

Land and power, family relations and love were, then, frequently exchanged or performed through the giving and receiving of gifts. Chapters 1 and 2 explored relationships between gods and humans through the lens of holy offerings, divine authority and narratives of sacrifice; I now want to expand on the importance of exchange in religious texts and through their circulation, using Islamic and Christian examples. The Qur'an's teachings and early Islamic traditions highlight the importance of generous giving and its harvest: 'Those who spend their wealth in God's cause are like the grains of corn that produce seven ears, each bearing a hundred grains.'[43] The value of generosity and hospitality has remained central to Islamic teaching and practice since then, both through examples in the Qur'an and in subsequent narratives and traditions. MS. Arab. c. 75 contains an extract from the Qur'an written in a beautiful Kufic script (figure 3.7). This passage is part of the story of Solomon and the Queen of Sheba, told in different versions in Jewish and Christian traditions too. The Queen reflects on a threatening message from Solomon, and decides to send him gifts as a response. Solomon derides the objects in comparison to Allah's gifts, and questions the motivations of her ambassadors. The story shows gift-exchange as central to statecraft, but then overturns that perspective to stress the unending generosity and power of Allah, whose spiritual gifts are also praised in Islamic medieval mystical poetry.[44] Passages such as this describe and reflect on acts of giving, but the books themselves can also be the focus of many kinds of exchange. For example, the gorgeous decorative designs in MS. Bodl. Or. 793, a sixteenth-century copy of the Qur'an written in Safavid Iran (figure 3.8), mark this book as owned or commissioned by a royal or noble reader. Across different religious cultures, precious books like this become a form of God-inspired gift that brings the reader closer to the divine, and also form part of royal collections that are exchanged, traded

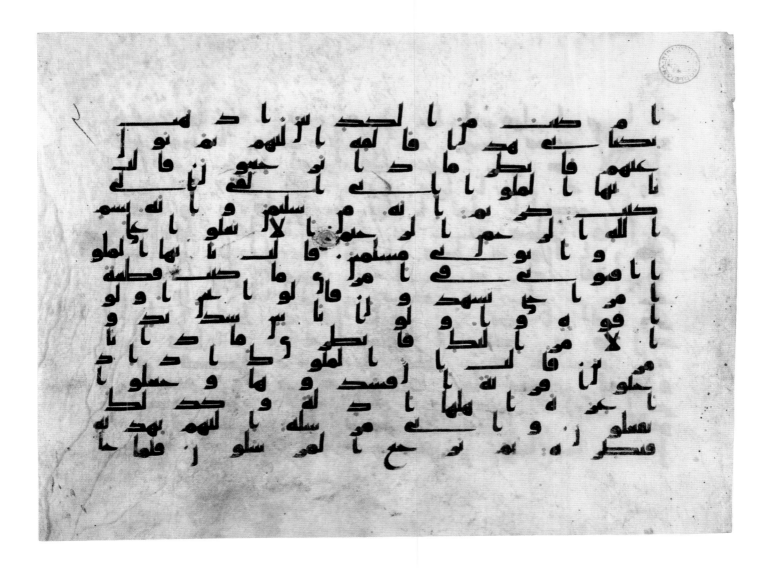

or seized. This book later belonged to Tipu Sultan, who ruled the Kingdom of
Mysore (based in South India) 1782–99. He conquered surrounding lands and
took their rulers' libraries into his own, exchanged gifts with numerous other
kingdoms, including the Ottoman Empire and rulers in Persia and Oman,
and allied with revolutionary France against the British. An automaton that
he commissioned, showing a tiger mauling a European soldier, is now on
display in the Victoria and Albert Museum in London, having been taken
from Tipu's capital Seringapatam, along with books such as this one, after the
British East India Company army besieged and looted it.[45]

3.7 An extract from the Qur'an written in
Kufic script, a style of writing frequently
used in the early Islamic period for holy
texts and architectural decoration. Oxford,
Bodleian Library, MS. Arab. c. 75, fol. 3a(i)
(Iraq, eighth or ninth century CE).

The Qur'an's teachings about generosity, and the fact that it is itself described as a divinely given revelation, help make its very nature resonant with the dynamics of give and take between humans and the divine discussed in Chapters 1 and 2. Christian narratives too use moments of giving to bring humans closer to God. In one richly illustrated Armenian gospel book (figure 3.9, and compare figure 0.1) this special kind of exchange is emphasized by paired illustrations of Magi from far-flung lands bringing gifts, and shepherds and animals offering their adoration to Jesus.[46] These acts of giving are part of an expanding network of exchange in Christian theology, stretching from God's creation and the duties that it places on humans in return, to the gift of the Incarnation of Christ, to the sacrifice and redemption (literally 'buying back') that Jesus enacts by being crucified. The complexity of these networks is shown in a beautifully illustrated opening from the *pars Aestivalis* (Summer part) of the Abingdon Missal (the *pars Hiemalis* is now in Trinity College, Oxford) (figure 3.10). The Crucifixion is depicted as a moment of pain, but also as a supreme act of generosity to humans by Christ as part of the Trinity (depicted as God the Father with the Holy Spirit as a dove near Christ's nimbed head), since his sacrificial body and blood will form the nurturing bread and wine of the Mass. These pages mark the start of the Canon of the Catholic Mass, where the priest asks God to bless the bread and wine, calling them *dona*, *munera*, *sancta sacrificia* (gifts; presents; holy sacrifices). On the right-hand page, the initial letter T of this prayer is illuminated with a picture of Abraham and Isaac, a red angel stopping the father from killing his son at the crucial moment when Abraham's obedience to God's command – his willingness to sacrifice his own child – has been verified. Christian theologians saw this story as a powerful foreshadowing of the Crucifixion. These pages also contain a donor figure at the left, wearing a mitre and the robes of the Benedictine order. His coat of arms, along with those of Abingdon Abbey, identify him as William Ashenden, Abbot of Abingdon from *c*.1436 to 1468. His presence at the centre of the manuscript's Christian story emphasizes the value of his sponsorship of this book. The speech scroll curling up from him in prayer translates as 'We adore you, Christ, and we bless you because through your holy Cross you redeemed the World.'

This moment of gift and sacrifice encapsulates the complex interplay of humility and attention-seeking that are so often mingled in medieval donor portraits. A much smaller, but still lavish, example comes in

3.8 Inside the roundels on these intricately decorated pages are written the first verses of the Qur'an, the lettering skilfully woven into the overall design. Oxford, Bodleian Library, MS. Bodl. Or. 793, fols. 9b–10a (Iran, 1550 CE).

Ծնունդն տեառն մերոյ Յիսուսի · յայրին բեթղեհեմի · որ եւ հովիւքն
[illegible] · գառն ընծայ անմահի գառինն [illegible]
[illegible] :

գ ասուաս սի Թազու որաշնե եմասու գանես գեն ձայան
ևորասնե սի եասասնան Թազու օրէս յիշի :

3.9 These striking Armenian gospel illustrations emphasize the comparison between the Magi and the shepherds arriving to worship and bring gifts to the newborn Jesus. The artist is the highly accomplished Mesrop of Khizan. Oxford, Bodleian Library, MS. Arm. d. 13, fols. 3v–4r (Armenia, 1609).

Te igitur cle
mentissime
pater per ihm
xpm filium
tuum dium no
strum. supplices rogamus
et petimus. uti accepta habeas
et benedicas ✠ hec ✠ dona.
✠ hec ✠ munera. ✠ hec ✠
sancta sacrificia illibata. In
primis que tibi offerimus pro
ecclesia tua sancta catholica. quā
pacificare custodire adunare. et
regere digneris toto orbe terrar
una cum famulo tuo Rege nro

previous pages **3.10** Along with its donor portrait, the intricate illustrations on these pages of the Abingdon Missal link the Crucifixion to the story of Abraham and Isaac as moments of offering and sacrifice. Oxford, Bodleian Library, MS. Digby 227, fols 113v–114r (England (perhaps Oxford), 1461).

right **3.11** Jeanne de Baillencourt kneels in prayer, with the Virgin Mary and baby Jesus part of the same interior space, in a scene that is both intimate and alludes to wider cycles of salvation. Oxford, Bodleian Library, MS. Rawl. liturg. f. 33, fol. 174v (Belgium, 1566).

opposite **3.12** This page from the Ormesby Psalter teems with life and colour, from the sleeping Jesse at its foot, to two sets of donor figures, to the prophets, Virgin Mary and Christ and right up to angel musicians. Oxford, Bodleian Library, MS. Douce 366, fol. 9v (England (East Anglia), originally later 1200s; altered in the 1300s).

MS. Rawlinson liturg. f. 33 (figure 3.11), in which a female owner/donor is portrayed with her prayer book (perhaps that book itself) open, and another on the floor in front of her. She faces the reader, perhaps inviting the viewer (including her future self) to emulate the vision of elegant piety she portrays, though her insistent presence also complicates our view of the Virgin Mary and baby Jesus. The portrait is of Jeanne de Baillencourt, viscomtesse de Hanicamp, and the manuscript was made for her at Bois-Seigneur-Isaac Abbey (in modern Belgium) in 1566. Mary, breastfeeding Jesus, has been brought into a domestic space, with little to mark a boundary between Jeanne and the holy pair, and playing on the particular intimacy that a female donor may have with Mary as mother. But this is not merely a cosy picture of mutually satisfying nurture exchanged in milk, prayer and blessing: with the help of a hovering angel, Jesus holds the Cross, while another angel crowns Mary Queen of Heaven. The picture is a complex and shifting scene in which the gifts of love, prayer and sacrifice are echoed by their homecoming or repayment. Likewise, Jeanne de Baillencourt's commissioning of this manuscript binds her into relationships that are both gift-orientated and economic or self-interested: with the abbey and with the belief that prayer and religious patronage can store up credit for the afterlife.

Many gifts move, and set other exchanges in motion too, but some precious objects are removed from circulation and become integral to the family or institution that holds them (what the anthropologist Annette Weiner termed 'keeping-while-giving').[47] A spectacular example that illustrates both continuity and adaptation is the Ormesby Psalter, first written and illustrated in East Anglia in the later 1200s, but altered more than once during the 1300s (figure 3.12). The psalm text starts with a huge initial 'B' for *Beatus* (Blessed), the first word of the Latin psalms, which almost disappears amidst the flourishing tendrils of a Jesse tree, with the biblical Jesse asleep at the foot of the page and his descendants in roundels formed by the branches stemming from his loins. The noble inheritance of Christ is interlaced with two donor figures: a boy from the Foliot family (perhaps Richard (d. 1325 aged 14)), and a girl from the Bardolf family, who were possibly to be married. They kneel in prayer, looking up to Christ himself crowning Mary near the top of the page. However, below the first line of text, the sinuous decoration is interrupted by two squares of stippled gold, where two new donors are pictured, rivalling even Jesse for size. These are a bishop (almost certainly of Norwich), and Robert of Ormesby

(d. ?1350s), himself a monk but also a wealthy patron paying for this re-donation and additional illustrations throughout the book. Through his gift he no doubt hoped to gain thanks and benefits from the priory and from Christ himself. The new portraits literally block out the rest of the text, which is accommodated on a new *Beatus* scheme on the next page. It is possible that this manuscript was connected with Norwich Priory from its first creation through several updates and sponsored 'refreshes'.[48] Like a cathedral attracting donors for new building work across many generations, this monumental book suggests how gifts can forge new relationships and change their meaning without even needing to travel in space.

Debating and debasing the gift

The Ormesby Psalter is one of the most sumptuous examples of regifting from the Bodleian's collections, but the complex ethics of giving – how far gifts were really altruistic, or whether an agreement to exchange should always be upheld – have been the subject of frequent debate. Chapter 4 discusses early modern responses to these questions, but they are also at the heart of the brilliant fourteenth-century poem *Sir Gawain and the Green Knight*. Amidst the traditional New Year's gift-exchange at King Arthur's court, a huge and uncanny Green Knight rides into the hall, and challenges Arthur to a game: an exchange of blows. Gawain asks to take up the challenge and cuts off the Green Knight's head, but he strides over, picks it up and it speaks, warning Gawain that he faces payback in a year's time. Having set off to fulfil his duty, Gawain rests at the house of the genial Bertilak and they agree that over the next few days they will exchange whatever they gain. Bertilak brings back the kill from his hunting, while Gawain plays a dangerously flirtatious game with his host's unnamed wife, and ceremoniously passes onto Bertilak the mounting number of kisses he receives from her. An illustration in the unique manuscript (figure 3.13) vividly captures the power and threat that Bertilak's wife exerts over Gawain, in the curtained enclosure of his bed, during their intricate verbal and physical exchanges. Finally, Gawain accepts a belt which, she claims, will magically protect him. Instead of offering this to Bertilak, Gawain conceals it. He thinks he can now emerge unscathed, but it's he who has been played: the Green Knight is also Bertilak, and knows about Gawain's dishonesty. He sends Gawain back to Arthur with wounds to his neck and

right **3.13** Gawain pretends to sleep while his host Bertilak's wife strokes his chin, ready for a dangerous game of flirtation in the famous fourteenth-century poem *Sir Gawain and the Green Knight*. In the text, she teasingly asks whether he really is the legendary Gawain if he's not willing to make love to her. London, British Library, Cotton MS. Nero A.x, fol. 129r (England, *c*. 1400).

opposite **3.14** In Thomas Hoccleve's poem *The Regiment of Princes* (1410–11), the impecunious and anxious poet claims that his advice on rulership to Prince Henry (later Henry V) is a form of generous gift, hoping that the prince will in turn reward him. London, British Library, Royal MS 17. D. 6, fol. 40r (England, between 1425 and 1450).

ye and noble prince excellent
My lord the prince, my lord gracious
I humble servaunt and obedient
Unto your estate hye and glorious
Of whiche I am full tendir and full ielous
Me recommaunde unto your worthynesse
With hert entier and spirite of mekenesse

pride, while forgiving with a laugh the knight's instinct to save his skin. The poem places the absolute claims of chivalric honour and religious morality against the many subtle shades of give and take in relations amongst men, women, values, beliefs and communities. The resulting debate, not only in Arthur's court but amongst the poem's audience, still continues.

Debating gifts and exchange in any court, whether that was Camelot or Westminster, required writers to tread a delicate line between the moral case for charity, the need for rulers to be both munificent and prudent, and the potentially explosive messages of the New Testament on riches and poverty. Most advisory texts praised generosity and humility (including, of course, accepting advice), but also stressed the need to be canny and avoid being conned by flatterers into needless extravagance or 'foole largesse'. Thomas Hoccleve (d. 1426), addressing the future Henry V in his advice poem *The Regiment of Princes*, had a particularly narrow path to navigate. In an opening autobiographical dialogue with an old man he meets, Thomas laments his debilitating anxiety and lack of funds (Hoccleve was a government clerk in the Privy Seal Office in Westminster, whose pay was often delayed). The dialogue reveals Thomas's poverty, exposes some of the tensions at the heart of England's governance, and becomes an application for the job of advice poet – a role that the old man presses him to take up, saying that Prince Henry is bound to reward him for this valuable service. Hoccleve then addresses the prince, describing himself as poor in money but rich in goodwill ('Thogh that my lyflode and possessioun / Be scant, I ryche am of benevolence'), and so imagining himself as a generous giver of advice to Henry.[49] One copy of the *Regiment* in the British Library (figure 3.14) includes a picture showing a poet with a prominent but presumably empty purse, offering his book as a gift to the dominant prince. The fiction that this relationship is one of freely given advice is important to maintaining its decorum, but is severely pressurized by imbalances of power and status. Many books in this period were written to order, or to nourish patronage relations, and so writers were acutely aware of the rhetoric of deferential address, and the fear of irritating the powerful audiences on whose generosity they relied.

Hoccleve's *Regiment* yearns for a ruler who can regulate his own desires and keep a healthy body politic in balance. However, in pandemic-ravaged England accusations of hypocrisy and corruption in high places were rife. William Langland's poem *Piers Plowman* (written and revised

3.15 Lady Meed, the embodiment of corruption in William Langland's poem *Piers Plowman*, is carried by a sheriff. Her crown and elegant dress indicate her aspirations to grandeur. She carries a cup, possibly a chalice or one of those she promises to distribute to her followers in return for favours. Oxford, Bodleian Library, MS. Douce 104, fol. 10r (Dublin, *c.* 1420).

163

170

10

þo lende þey hem to westmynstre þno weddyng to hono[ur]
at hakeneo had þai none but hakeneyes to hyre
þan gan gyle to borow horsse at many gret mayster[es]
and schop þat a schyef þold bey mede
softely in sambue þo sase to aise
and false and fauel feyth forþe sas[e]
and þde fory on hem & on reueo wyth fast by mede
symony and syvile seyde and sworen
þat þstes & þisoo schuld plateo eque
and y my silf syuile and symony my felell
wol þde a þon serteo & pth me anoutoyo
and notaryes and þsoues þat þuute oft
and þore þisoo and a þeleo i þe eyþeo
sompueo & sydeueo þat supsedias takey
on hem y touey techury lepyn up & rydyn
on executeo and euth me touey sost aftey
and let cope þe cosayp þey tost sthal he shall
and fetten our uitayleo ou formeateo
and maken on þey a sous caye to lede al þoo oy
as falsoo and fayroo þat ou þey fete þyuuey
þan false and fauel rydyn fory to gydeyo
and mede in þe myddes & al þoo men aftyr
I haue no toug to tel þe tayl y þam folollbey
of many maw me for mede is sabe is sent aft[er]
gyle was forgoey to gydyn al þoo þeynl
for to þeir þam wey and wyþ mede a byde
sopeueo taugh þam al and sud but litil
and prikked fory on pateuo & passed þe all
and come to þe kynges courte & consteuo told
and consteuo to þe kyng trypyd þis aftyr
noll be crist goo þe kyng and y catch myzt
falso oy fauel or hey falell þey
y wold be a wyeke on þo eweyschee & on þey weyeo al
and to þem þeug by þe halse & al þ þam meytauey
sthal neuey man on þo wolde maynþrise þe lest

c. 1360s–1380s) is a dream vision whose protagonist Will asks the question 'How can I be saved?'. One answer is by the gift of God's grace. But this world is full of sin: our own, of course, but also that of hypocritical friars who grow rich despite being a mendicant (begging) order, and greedy courtiers who will turn a blind eye if the incentives are right. Joyously embodying the perversion of gift into bribe is the personified figure of Meed (a word whose meaning ranges across reward, payment and bribe). She brazenly offers cups, rings and cash to gain influence at court, and agrees with a friar to donate to his church if he absolves her sins. She is brought before the king, who asks Conscience (another allegorical personification) if he will marry her, but he refuses, castigating the way she 'lereth hem lecherye that louyeth here yeftes … She hath apoisend popes, she appeyreth holy churche' (*teaches lechery to those who love her gifts … She has poisoned popes, she damages Holy Church*).[50] Meed encapsulates the problem with gifts: in a perfectly balanced world, why should we need the surplus of the gift? But if gifts oil the workings of life, when does a tip become a bribe, and is there anything that shouldn't be given or sold? An early fifteenth-century copy of *Piers Plowman* illustrates Meed in various colourful guises; in one picture (figure 3.15) she is carried to court on the shoulders of a sheriff – someone who should uphold the law, but actually relies on backhanders to provide money for his fine robe.

Langland's contemporary Geoffrey Chaucer created perhaps the best-known figures in medieval literature to represent the confusing possibilities of gift and requital: the pilgrim company of *The Canterbury Tales*. Meeting at the Tabard Inn in Southwark, across the Thames from London, they form a microcosm of social relations and an economy powered by the exchange of stories. Here, too, friars come under particular scrutiny. *The Summoner's Tale* satirizes a corrupt friar who preaches hellfire and damnation, frightening people into giving him money in exchange for prayers for their departed relatives. The friar's sidekick notes down the donors' names on a wax tablet, but when they leave town he wipes it clean:

> He planed awey the names everichon   *smoothed away*
> That he biforn had writen in his tables;   *before, writing tablets*
> He served hem with nyfles and with fables.[51]   *palmed them off*
>   *with tricks and lies*

Our last comment on the complexities of medieval giving goes to a man in the tale named Thomas, lying sick in bed. The friar butters up Thomas's wife with airy talk about the power of mendicant prayers and then turns to Thomas himself, hoping for a fat donation. Thomas asks the friar to put his hand down underneath his backside, where he is keeping 'A thyng that I have hyd in pryvetee' (3.2143), on condition that he divides it equally amongst his fellow friars. The friar eagerly explores: 'And doun his hand he launcheth to the clifte [crack] / In hope for to fynde there a yifte' (3.2145–6). Thomas's gift is in an unexpected currency, though:

> Amydde his hand he leet the frere a fart;
> There nys no capul, drawynge in a cart,
> That myghte have lete a fart of swich a soun. (3.2149–51)
> (*Right on his hand he gave the friar a fart; there's no horse,*
> *pulling a cart, that could have let go a fart with such a sound.*)

Outraged, the friar demands vengeance from the local lord, but the insult is laughed off, except for pondering the scientific challenge of dividing the fart's sound and smell equally amongst the group of friars: this is described as a devilish problem of 'ars-metrike' (3.2222). Thomas's fart is a satirical comment on the dark underbelly of gift relations in medieval Britain, but is also a gift for a storyteller like Chaucer, echoing out to the competitive story-exchange that structures *The Canterbury Tales*, and beyond to Chaucer's audience, in shock, laughter and debate.

Reaching from pre-Conquest gifts of land which writing both describes and ratifies, through the urgent exchanges of lovers, the give and take of patrons, owners and scribes, the value of stories for wisdom and instruction, and the corruption of gifts in late-medieval court and Church, books and gifts are, then, intimately and subtly bound together in medieval cultures. Fortunately for us, those reciprocal relations leave many traces in the objects, books and stories still preserved in the Bodleian and beyond.

The Byble in Englyſhe, that is to ſaye the content of all the holy ſcrypture, bothe of ẏ olde and newe teſtament, truly tranſlated after the veryte of the Hebrue and Greke textes, by ẏ dylygent ſtudye of dyuerſe excellent learned men, expert in the forſayde tonges.

Prynted by Rychard Grafton & Edward Whitchurch.

Cum priuilegio ad imprimendum ſolum.

1539.

Chapter 4

Gifts and Exchange in Early Modern Society

Felicity Heal

In early modern Britain, gifts were bound into all kinds of social interaction. They were integral to formal occasions that expressed hierarchies and political allegiances; they were an everyday aspect of family and working life at many levels; and they were a subject for teaching, theorizing and debate. Books themselves could be magnificent gifts, but they could also reflect on the potential of giving to refashion social relationships, for better or worse. In this chapter I trace some of those interactions and reflections, whether at the royal court, amongst scholars and patrons, or between and within families.

Crown and court: the reign of Elizabeth

On 14 January 1559, the day before her coronation, Elizabeth I made her ceremonial entry into the city of London. The occasion was marked by elaborate rituals of welcome, with dramatic scenes punctuating the route, and a number of carefully staged exchanges of praise and gratitude between people and queen. The author of the description chose, however, to privilege two moments in this rich ceremony: the queen's entry into the Tower of London, where she expressed gratitude for her delivery from its 'cruel den' in the previous reign of Mary her half-sister, and her acceptance of a Bible in English at the pageant in Cheapside. Elizabeth is described as taking the scriptures in both hands and promising the city fathers that she would 'read it most diligently'.[52] This was taken as crucial evidence that the new queen was turning away from Mary's Catholicism, with its scepticism about the vernacular Bible, and towards some sort of reformed faith. Historians have long debated the sort of religious settlement Elizabeth would have preferred, and her own beliefs. It is, however, incontrovertible that the scriptures in English were a keystone of Elizabeth's rejection of papal Catholicism, and an expression of the bond between Crown and people. This is most powerfully expressed in the frontispieces of the public Tudor Bibles: the 1539 Great Bible (figure 4.1) and the Bishops' Bible of

4.1 Frontispiece of the first official English-language Bible, the Great Bible, 1539. Henry VIII, like a latter-day Moses, hands the volume to his loyal subjects. Oxford, Bodleian Library, Bib. Eng. 1539 b.1.

1568. In 1539 Henry VIII is displayed in full imperial majesty, giving the scripture to his lay and clerical elite, who then provide it to the people. They thank Henry, not God, their speech scrolls calling out 'vivat rex' ([*long*] *live the King*). The Bishops' Bible has a less assertive image. It shows a portrait of the queen surrounded by the virtues of faith, hope and charity in classical garb. It still claims that Elizabeth is the upholder of the Word of God, which is being preached to a devout congregation at the foot of the page.[53] When the queen received the Bible as a gift, as she often did as part of traditional New Year gift exchanges, it served as a reminder of her commitment to ground her religious policies in God's Word.

The political use of the English Bible was integral to a culture laden with ideas of gift exchange. In practice, monarchs determined what should be imposed upon the people, but the classical values of beneficence and liberality, accompanied by a prudential need for political control, meant that the Crown often presented religious changes as gifted to their subjects. And much other exchange between ruler and ruled was also 'enchanted' through mutual giving. This can be seen very clearly at the royal progresses that were a characteristic of the sixteenth century, and especially of Elizabeth's reign. The queen used her visits to noble households and to cities as a way of showing her approbation of her leading subjects, as well as saving court costs during the summer. The elites in turn showered her with pageants and gifts both to demonstrate loyalty and to remind the monarch of their political and material needs. Elizabeth's 1566 visit to the University of Oxford shows this process at work: the queen attended a carefully chosen set of plays and disputations, the latter being geared to questions of obedience, rather than to contentious religious issues. Town and gown both gave predictable gifts of silver and jewels, but there was also a more distinctive present of pictures of the colleges and accompanying verses from John Bereblock and Thomas Neale (figure 4.2). This offered more than a stylish gift: it implied the generally conservative religious attitude of many of the academics, a reminder that it would not be easy to convert her older university to enthusiasm for Protestantism. In the later Elizabethan progresses, especially those of the 1590s, the requests of her subjects were often hidden in symbols and allegory. Now the queen was woven into the drama, and dramatization, of the visit: jewels were offered to her by singing shepherds, elegant clothing by wild men.[54] This became the world of the court masque, a more familiar feature of the

4.2 The Divinity School of the University of Oxford, illustrated in John Bereblock and Thomas Neale, 'A welcoming dialogue for the visit of the Queen, the most serene Lady Elizabeth', *c.* 1566, commemorating Elizabeth I's visit to the University. Oxford, Bodleian Library, MS. Bodl. 13, part 1, fol. 16v.

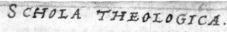

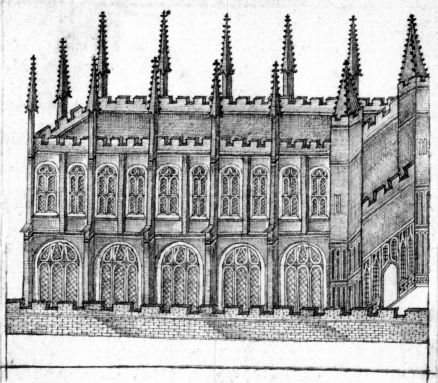

Cansell. *E minet, & mediæ fastigia suspirit vrbis,*

    Dux Humfrede, tuis sumptibus ista schola.

Surgit in immensum turritis vndiq; pinnis.

    Sertaq; perpulchro marmore,quadra domus.

Splendida luminibus crebris laquearia fulgent,

    Artificiumq; nitent pendula saxa manu.

Cœpit sub Henrico. 6° per dominum Humfredum
Ducem Glorestriæ. Anno domini.   1441.

TO OVR MOST NOBLE AND
vertuous quene KATHERIN, Eliza
beth, her humble daughter wisheth:
perpetuall felicitie and everlasting ioye

NOT ONELY knowing the affe
ctuous wille, and feruent zeale, the
wich your highnes hath towardes
all godly lerning, as alſo my dutie
towardes you (most gracious and ſo
uerain *prince*) but knowing alſo that
puſilanimite and ydlenes are moſt
repugnante vnto a reaſonable crea
ture: and that (as the philoſopher
ſayeth) euen as an inſtrument of yron

previous pages **4.3** and **4.4**
The laboriously made cover and dedication page of Princess Elizabeth's translation of Marguerite of Navarre's *The Miroir or Glasse of the Synnefull Soule*, a New Year's gift to her stepmother Queen Katherine Parr, 1544. Oxford, Bodleian Library, MS. Cherry 36, upper cover; fol. 2r.

4.5 This impressive copy of the Geneva Bible, with decorative gold top, bottom and fore-edges and an embroidered cover incorporating a Tudor rose, was presented to Queen Elizabeth I at New Year 1584 by her printer Christopher Barker. Oxford, Bodleian Library, Bib. Eng. 1583 b.1.

Stuart regimes, in which the affirmation of royal authority was disguised by enchanted fictions.

Loyalty was also performed through gifting, a common feature of early modern courts that Henry VIII and his younger daughter eagerly encouraged. Princess Elizabeth, surviving in the dangerous world created by her father, used gifts from early youth as a way of expressing identity and forging alliances. And it is predictable that, given her outstanding education steeped in new humanist scholarship, she should turn to books as her means of communication. Her New Year gifts included her translation, in 1544, of Marguerite of Navarre's *The Miroir or Glasse of the Synnefull Soule*, given to Henry's last wife, Katherine Parr (figures 4.3 and 4.4). The gift had a threefold resonance: it showed the princess's skills in learning and in needlework; it identified her with the religious reformist group at court; and it thanked her stepmother for kindness in giving her protection and support. Once she came to the throne Elizabeth herself became the

focus for giving and exchange, especially at the New Year, celebrated with great ceremony in the Tudor court. Her nobles and courtiers were expected to perform their allegiance publicly at this gift-giving time, and to offer according to their status and favour. Those closest to the queen offered most. In 1588, for example, Sir Christopher Hatton gave a necklace and earrings so splendid that they needed fourteen lines of inventory to catalogue them. In return all givers were rewarded with carefully calibrated gold and silver: Hatton's haul in 1588 was 400 ounces of silver-gilt plate.[55] Such ceremonious and rich giving was a part of the courtly dance that the queen nurtured as a necessary aspect of her power and control. Lesser men and women could also participate, especially at New Year, either appealing to Elizabeth's well-known enthusiasm for elegant clothing or offering books as a way to praise her learning (figure 4.5). Elizabeth also showed her mastery of gift exchange on less ritual occasions: even a small gift, of limited intrinsic value, had to be treated ceremoniously. In one instance in 1595, the queen's secretary of state, Robert Cecil, presented her with three partridges killed by his hawks. Elizabeth insisted that they were passed to her ailing courtier Sir William More, and not saved for the royal table. But though she had redirected, rather than initiated, this gift, both More and Cecil were required to offer elaborate praise of her generosity. She was the fount of largesse, the centre of all court exchange. Elizabeth was at the heart of giving, receiving and ensuring thanks, sometimes identifying herself with the Three Graces of classical myth – who move in a continuous circle exchanging reward, benefit and gratitude. In *The Shepheardes Calender* (1579), the poet Edmund Spenser represented her in exactly this way: Elizabeth appears as a fourth Grace whose generosity is able 'to make the daunce even'.[56]

Understanding the gift economy

The sixteenth century saw new and more nuanced ways in which cultural behaviour involving friendship, generosity and exchange were expressed. Humanist scholars committed to the revitalization of classical learning saw the writers of Greece and Rome as providing templates for contemporary culture. The central figure of this northern Renaissance was Erasmus of Rotterdam (1466–1536). Erasmus was the international academic networker *par excellence*, a man who endeavoured to create a fellowship of the learned, bonded by correspondence, by the exchange of texts and by the patronage of fellow travellers (figure 4.6). Men of kindred spirit could not always be together, but through their shared intellectual pursuits they could participate in a community of equals. Sometimes Erasmus focused on material expressions of friendship. He exchanged portraits with patrons such as the Archbishop of Canterbury, William Warham, and sympathetic colleagues like Thomas More. He expected patronage to include attractive gifts and the offer of support. At other times he evoked the delight in social exchange that simply involved shared understanding, as in the dialogues in his *Colloquies* when feasts are imagined as food for the spirit. The giving and dedication of books performed these engagements in particularly powerful ways. For example, presenting his *Praise of Folly* (1511) to More (the title puns on the Latin word for foolish – *morus*), Erasmus writes, 'accept this as token for your friend and take it under your immediate protection'.[57]

The ideal of learned friendship within a community of scholars was also defined by the exclusion of those who challenged its values. Erasmus's correspondence is full of enemies made and denounced, from those who denied patronage to him and his friends, to those who were hostile to the new forms of classical learning. In his *Adages*, those maxims of wisdom learned by every Tudor schoolboy, generosity and the bond it created were praised – 'in gifts it is the spirit that matters'. However, these proverbs also suggest an anxiety about transactions that depended on social bonding. There are dangers in 'false gifts', especially when offered by flatterers and poets, and inequality in exchange produces enemies. Consideration of the virtues of generosity and largesse had long had an undertow of caution of this kind: the gifts of enemies could readily be dismissed as poisonous; yet accepting favours from friends could still be a burden to the recipient – 'who takes courtesy of another sells his liberty'.[58] The political environment of Renaissance Europe brought these moral considerations into sharper focus: the question of how to behave in court and city became more urgent. Humanist writers turned to the classics to find proper advice on these matters. Most often they turned to Roman authors, especially Cicero and Seneca, who had themselves wrestled with these issues in the competitive world of the Republic and then Empire. What was the proper form of the *vita activa* (the active life lived in court or city)? What were the obligations of the generous man and how did he discharge them honourably and yet with prudence? Cicero's *De amicitia* and *De officiis* (*On Friendship* and *On Duties*), and Seneca's *De beneficiis* (*On Benefits*) were the core books that

4.6 Desiderius Erasmus, the greatest of the Northern European humanists. This is a copy of the famous portrait by Hans Holbein. Erasmus's hands rest on a copy of one of his major scholarly achievements: his edition of the New Testament. Oxford, Bodleian Library, LP 26 (England, 1580–1600).

2. ...

... C. p. 293.

Douce
S. 207.

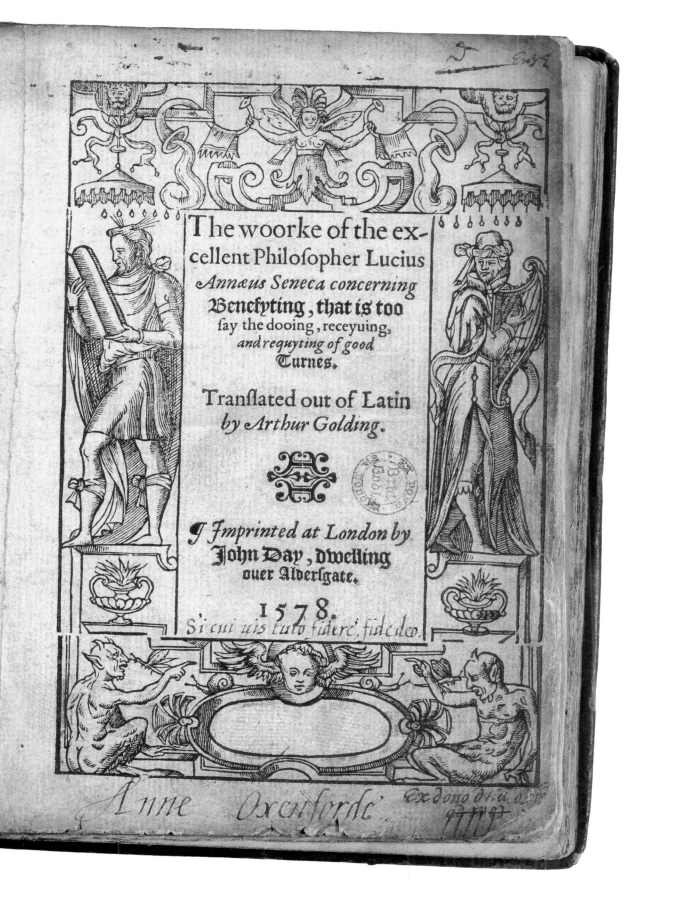

The woorke of the ex-
cellent Philosopher Lucius
Annæus Seneca concerning
Benefyting, that is too
say the dooing, receyuing,
and requyting of good
Turnes.

Translated out of Latin
by Arthur Golding.

¶ Imprinted at London by
John Day, dwelling
ouer Aldersgate.

1578.
Si cui uis tuto fidere, fide deo.

addressed these questions. While all three had much influence on the social behaviour of their Renaissance readers, it is Seneca who offers the most explicit guidance to the management of the gift economy.

Seneca's moral guidance was already well known before *De beneficiis* was translated into English. Juan Vives, in his *Introduction to Wisdome* (trans. 1540), used Seneca for a discussion of the spirit of giving; Thomas Wilson's *Art of Rhetorique* (1554) turned to Seneca to examine how and with whom favours should be exchanged. From Thomas Elyot's *The Boke of the Governour* (1531) to Richard Brathwaite's *The English Gentleman* (1630), advice given to gentlemen reflected aspects of Seneca, stressing the 'reciprocal courtesy' that should be the foundation of true society. 'Bounty', says Brathwaite, 'is a motive to love; for giving gifts gathereth friends'. In 1578 this influence was augmented when Arthur Golding provided the first full translation of *De beneficiis*, to be followed half a century later by Thomas Lodge's version. In the Bodleian's two copies of Golding's translation, many key passages are underlined by early readers, and one includes approving marginal notes throughout the first few books (figure 4.7).[59] So what did this reader and other contemporaries learn from Seneca's moralizing? Above all that the circulation of benefits, and their proper use, were of key importance in public life. Those benefits could be material – gifts great and small – or 'good deeds' undertaken in the proper spirit: 'for the good turne consisteth not in the thing that is doon or given but in the verye intent [real intention] of the dooer or giver'.[60] The personal relationship that underpinned this benevolence ensured that the gift was distinct from a commodity given a monetary value and exchanged in the market. So much for the ideal: the practice of Tudor politics demanded a more worldly-wise approach – one that Seneca expanded on later in *De beneficiis*. The giver must avoid excess or being too persistent while the recipient must avoid the sin of ingratitude.

Noble and gentry fathers sometimes presented Senecan advice to their sons as a guide to future conduct, but they had to balance the moral value of generosity and proper social bonding with reminders of how to promote their own interests. For example, William Cecil, Lord Burghley, advised his son Robert to maintain influence at court through small and regular gifts to great men, though the gift-giver should ensure that if any 'great gratuity' was presented it should be something that could be in daily sight: this would serve as a constant reminder to the recipient to be grateful.

previous pages **4.7** Arthur Golding's translation of the Roman moralist Seneca's work on gifts and benefits, 1578. This copy shows ownership marks and is extensively annotated. Oxford, Bodleian Library, Douce S 207, title page opening.

opposite **4.8** Shakespeare's *Timon of Athens*, 2.1.5–10 from the First Folio edition of Shakespeare's plays (1623). A senator comments on the profligate generosity of Timon, which is bound to lead to his ruin: 'It cannot hold, it will not'. Oxford, Bodleian Library, Arch. G c.7, fol. Gg4r.

Tim. Nay, and you begin to raile on Societie once, I
am sworne not to giue regard to you. Farewell, & come
with better Musicke.   *Exit*

Aper. So : Thou wilt not heare mee now, thou shalt
not then. Ile locke thy heauen from thee :
Oh that mens eares should be
To Counsell deafe, but not to Flatterie.   *Exit*

Enter a Senator.

Sen. And late fiue thousand : to *Varro* and to *Isidore*
He owes nine thousand, besides my former summe,
Which makes it fiue and twenty. Still in motion
Of raging waste? It cannot hold, it will not.
If I want Gold, steale but a beggers Dogge,
And giue it *Timon*, why the Dogge coines Gold.
If I would sell my Horse, and buy twenty moe
Better then he ; why giue my Horse to *Timon*.
Aske nothing, giue it him, it Foles me straight
And able Horses : No Porter at his gate,
But rather one that smiles, and still inuites
All that passe by. It cannot hold, no reason
Can sound his state in safety. *Caphis* hoa,
Caphis I say.

Enter Caphis.

Ca. Heere sir, what is your pleasure.
Sen. Get on your cloake, & hast you to Lord *Timon*,
Importune him for my Moneyes, be not ceast
With slight deniall ; nor then silenc'd, when
Commend me to your Master, and the Cap
Playes in the right hand, thus : but tell him,
My Vses cry to me ; I must serue my turne
Out of mine owne, his dayes and times are past,
And my reliances on his fracted dates
Haue smit my credit. I loue, and honour him,
But must not breake my backe, to heale his finger.
Immediate are my needs, and my releefe
Must not be tost and turn'd to me in words,
But finde supply immediate. Get you gone,
Put on a most importunate aspect,
A visage of demand : for I do feare
When euery Feather stickes in his owne wing,
Lord *Timon* will be left a naked gull,
Which flashes now a Phœnix, get you gone.
Ca. I go sir.
Sen. I go sir ?
Take the Bonds along with you,
And haue the dates in. Come.
Ca. I will Sir.
Sen. Go.   *Exeunt*

Enter Steward, with many billes in his hand.

Stew. No care, no stop, so senselesse of expence,
That he will neither know how to maintaine it,
Nor cease his flow of Riot. Takes no accompt
How things go from him, nor resume no care
Of what is to continue : neuer minde,
Was to be so vnwise, to be so kinde.
What shall be done, he will not heare, till feele :
I must be round with him, now he comes from hunting.
Fye, fie, fie, fie.

Enter Caphis, Isidore, and Varro.

Cap. Good euen *Varro* : what, you come for money?
Var. Is't not your businesse too?
Cap. It is, and yours too, *Isidore?*
Isid. It is so.

Cap. Would we were all discharg'd.
Var. I feare it,
Cap. Heere comes the Lord.

Enter Timon, and his Traines.

Tim. So soone as dinners done, wee'l forth againe
My *Alcibiades*. With me, what is your will?
Cap. My Lord, heere is a note of certaine dues.
Tim. Dues? whence are you?
Cap. Of Athens heere, my Lord.
Tim. Go to my Steward.
Cap. Please it your Lordship, he hath put me off
To the succession of new dayes this moneth :
My Master is awak'd by great Occasion,
To call vpon his owne, and humbly prayes you,
That with your other Noble parts, you'l suite,
In giuing him his right.
Tim. Mine honest Friend,
I prythee but repaire to me next morning.
Cap. Nay, good my Lord.
Tim. Containe thy selfe, good Friend.
Var. One *Varroes* seruant, my good Lord.
Isid. From *Isidore*, he humbly prayes your speedy pay-
ment.
Cap. If you did know my Lord, my Masters wants.
Var. 'Twas due on forfeyture my Lord, sixe weekes,
and past.
Isi. Your Steward puts me off my Lord, and I
Am sent expressely to your Lordship.
Tim. Giue me breath :
I do beseech you good my Lords keepe on,
Ile waite vpon you instantly. Come hither : pray you
How goes the world, that I am thus encountred
With clamorous demands of debt, broken Bonds,
And the detention of long since due debts
Against my Honor?
Stew. Please you Gentlemen,
The time is vnagreeable to this businesse :
Your importunacie cease, till after dinner,
That I may make his Lordship vnderstand,
Wherefore you are not paid.
Tim. Do so my Friends, see them well entertain'd.
Stew. Pray draw neere.   *Exit.*

Enter Apemantus and Foole.

Caph. Stay, stay, here comes the Foole with *Apeman-
tus*, let's ha some sport with 'em.
Var. Hang him, hee'l abuse vs.
Isid. A plague vpon him dogge.
Var. How dost Foole?
Ape. Dost Dialogue with thy shadow?
Var. I speake not to thee.
Ape. No 'tis to thy selfe. Come away.
Isi. There's the Foole hangs on your backe already.
Ape. No thou stand'st single, th'art not on him yet.
Cap. Where's the Foole now?
Ape. He last ask'd the question. Poore Rogues, and
Vsurers men, Bauds betweene Gold and want.
Al. What are we *Apemantus*?
Ape. Asses.
All. Why?
Ape. That you aske me what you are, & do not know
your selues. Speake to 'em Foole.
Foole. How do you Gentlemen?
All. Gramercies good Foole :
How does your Mistris?

                                                        Foole.

Henry Percy, ninth earl of Northumberland, warned his son Algernon that managing proper exchange required art: 'how to give, that yow may have the thanks … in it lyeth the mistery'.[61] The Tudor person in the street might encounter Senecan ideas via drama rather than print culture. Communities of exchange were often explored on the stage, and no one reflected more on their right use than Shakespeare. In *King Lear*, *The Merchant of Venice* and *Timon of Athens*, for example, he explores the nature of generosity, the proper understanding of community and the need to manage social relationships with prudence and caution. *Timon* addresses these ideas most directly: its protagonist gives with unstinted generosity to all comers and seems at first sight to embody the true spirit of beneficence (figure 4.8). He gives 'twenty-fold' as return when presents are given to him. But his largesse lacks discrimination and fails to establish true reciprocal relationships with those who receive his gifts. When his money runs out, he is destroyed by ingratitude, left bitter and friendless. He goes to live in a cave and gives a hoard of gold he finds to the exiled Alcibiades, who plans to march against Athens. Here, the consequences of excessive generosity and greed destabilize the state as a whole.

Givers and their gifts

Early modern English society has been characterized as a 'culture of giving', in which almost all social groups were enmeshed in the bonds of hospitality, liberality, friendship and charity. While Erasmus sometimes argued that full understanding of these virtues was the prerogative of the learned, he recognized that informal social networks, sustained by giving and receiving presents and benefits, were a common coin of everyday life. In the dedication of one of his *Colloquies* he noted that the 'homespun sort' cared about keeping affectionate relationships going when apart and did so by giving small material things such as rings, knives and caps.[62] The Herrick letters, a rich archive of a merchant clan that had members in Leicester and London, illustrate Erasmus's comment (figure 4.9). They are full of mentions of small gifts that were tokens of affection – knives, handkerchiefs, combs, many forms of food and even small books. Such gifts were not the sole, or even most important, way of expressing bonds of loyalty and affinity; however, material tokens do have a vital place in this culture, and when we can locate evidence of modest gifts among ordinary folk they are usually of this kind. Commitments of engagement to marry

Ryghard Hofeld I pray yow delyvr y baskyt y yone tak
to London of myne. to my sonne Nycolas Eyryk. at
Shew hym y I have sent vnto hym for a token ij doss
feldyfaris. for hym sellf and for hys suster mary. e for
hys brothar wyllm.

one doss bryds for hys brothar harvy e hys newe wiffe
one doss for hys brothar holdin e hys wiff
and one doss bryds for my cozin pegyn

From yowr fathez and mother
John Eyryk e mary

4.9 One of many letters, often accompanied by gifts, sent between Leicester and London by members of the Herrick family of merchants. Here, father John and mother Mary Herrick arrange for fieldfares to be sent as a gift of food to son Nicholas and his siblings and cousins in the capital. Oxford, Bodleian Library, MS. Eng. hist. c. 474, fol. 85r.

were marked by exchanges of tokens, some, especially the ring, having much the same central importance as in modern society (a sixteenth-century posy ring, possibly for an engagement, is illustrated in Chapter 3, figure 3.5). In Shakespeare's *The Merchant of Venice* (4.2), Portia seals her relationship to Bassanio by giving him a ring, 'which, when you part from, lose, or give away / Let it presage the ruin of your love'. Later, in disguise as the lawyer Balthazar, she plays a trick on him by demanding this ring as part payment for her services, and the question of rings, promises and the exchanges of love are central to the final scenes of the play. The evidence suggests that what was given at engagement or marriage was less important in itself than the signal of intent that the offering displayed. Church courts, asked to adjudicate promises to marry, took very seriously the gifts that were exchanged and the language that accompanied them. Rites of passage were supported by presents to the participants and witnesses, the latter often given gloves both at weddings and at funerals. These reflected the networks of support that family, neighbours and sometimes patrons gave

4.10 This set of platters, made in England *c.* 1590s, is elegantly decorated, each with a distinctive set of Old Testament verses. They could be read at a 'banquet': a light dessert of sweetmeats and fruits which became popular as after-dinner entertainment in wealthy Elizabethan households. They fit into a book-shaped box. Oxford, Ashmolean Museum, accession number AN2009. 6.

to ordinary people, the modest circulation of benefits that were a necessary part of everyday life.

The exchange of food provided a particularly strong affirmation of community. In the Herrick letters we can see that food was circulated within the family even more regularly than other commodities – this was partly to take advantage of things available in city or country, partly to show the practical affection of the matriarch of the family for her young, and partly because gifts of food were an important signal of shared breaking of bread even when distance precluded the reality of convivial eating. Food was one of the most fundamental ways in which networks of exchange were nurtured throughout the culture. Almost anyone could make a present of the produce of the land as a way to sustain social bonding. In Henry VIII's court little gifts of pears or apples from 'poor men' were deemed an acceptable offering at New Year. Tenants routinely produced gifts of game and poultry for the lord's table, though it is not always easy to distinguish free offerings from obligations. Contemporaries certainly saw the merits of bonding through food. William Perkins, an Elizabethan Puritan divine, advised a tenant to persuade a landlord to deal favourably with him by offering 'now and then a capon' or a pig or goose, while his wife should produce 'spiced cakes' and fruit for his lady.[63] Gifting among the elites also regularly involved food, especially if novelties such as unusual game or rare fruits could be provided for one's peers. Bonding through food was most resonant when it was demonstrated through hospitality. Royal feasts, tenant dinners at New Year, and guild celebrations in towns and cities were all major occasions for expressing people's identities and social relations. Even daily meals in the noble or gentry household were often open to all comers who could claim business or friendship, and served to define an affinity of supporters and associates. A set of decorated wooden platters in the Ashmolean Museum show that shared meals could involve the exchange of ideas as well as food (figure 4.10). Each platter includes a different cluster of Old Testament verses with moralizing themes. They seem to be designed to be read aloud as part of the evening's experience.

The book, whether printed or in manuscript, was a gift often deliberately set apart from everyday exchange. Authors used dedications to speak with deference of patrons, either those who had already given their blessing to a project or those who might give material support. The extension of print culture made such proclamations of deference commonplace, a routine

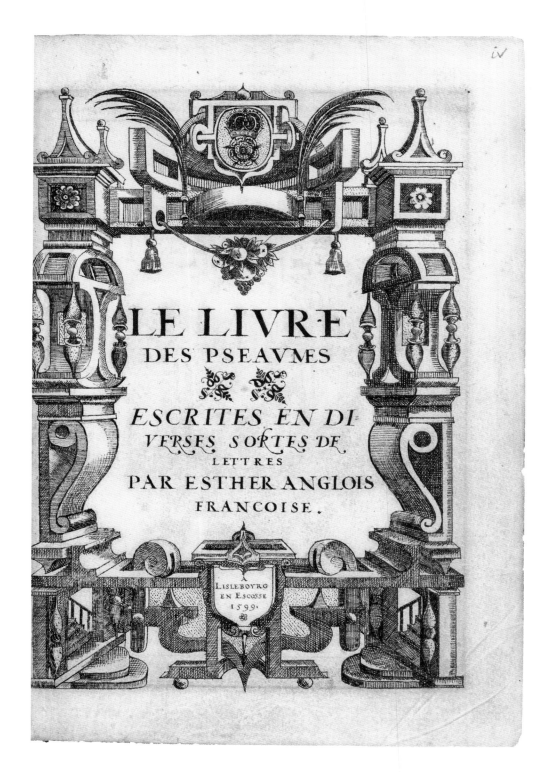

iv

4.11 The renowned scribe Esther Inglis copied this book of Psalms, handwritten in a variety of calligraphic styles, as a gift to Elizabeth I. Inglis hoped for reward and patronage in return. Oxford, Christ Church, MS. 180, fol. iv recto.

part of the community of the learned. No publication was deemed to be complete without claiming one or two people as sympathetic readers. Sometimes a whole community of the cognoscenti was invoked. Edmund Spenser opened the 1590 edition of the first three books of *The Faerie Queene* with a full 'letter' to Sir Walter Raleigh and no fewer than seventeen dedicatory sonnets addressed to the most elevated readers. This elaboration is an ambivalent way of claiming patrons, at once intimate and individual and publicly proclaimed to all readers. Spenser saw his work as a national epic, and so it needed to be addressed to the greatest in the realm. Yet even here there is the possibility of a greater or lesser expression of friendship: his sonnet of gratitude to Lord Grey, whom he served in Ireland, speaks with personal loyalty of this 'Patrone of my Muses pupillage', to whom he is 'bound … by vassalage', and who is now offered a 'small guift' in return.[64] Other writers eschewed print in favour of manuscript circulation, developing a group of privileged and sympathetic readers and avoiding the contamination of the public gaze. This was a particularly useful tactic if the recipient was the monarch. Lord Morley, for example, specialized in giving royalty from Henry VIII to Mary I handwritten New Year books of counsel. In another remarkable case the quality of the handwriting itself became the gift. These were gift-books copied by the Scottish-raised calligrapher Esther Inglis, for example a transcription of the Psalms in French (figure 4.11), which demonstrates Inglis's consummate skill, and which she and her husband Bartholomew Kello presented to Elizabeth in 1599.

Books had readers as well as authors and served to construct and develop communities. Literary exchanges among the educated flowed from the training they had received at university or their shared intellectual interests and became a major source of bonding. This might culminate in the public giving of knowledge, a process brilliantly exploited by Sir Thomas Bodley, who refounded the library that became the Bodleian. The weighty Donors' Book lists gifts of books to the library and honours the most important donors with prominent titles and coats of arms (figure 4.12). Books were also a means of sharing ideological commitments. A particularly vivid example is that of Sir Thomas Tresham, committed Catholic recusant and book collector, who labelled most of his volumes *Tresham et amicorum* ([property] of Tresham and friends) and provided access to his collections for like-minded sufferers for their faith. Or books could be a bond within a group of bibliophiles. Richard Stonley (*c*. 1520–1599), an Elizabethan

4.12 A page from the Bodleian Library's register of donors from 1607, showing the gift of Katharine Sandys, wife of Sir Edwin Sandys. The items bought with her £20 donation may reflect the family interest in exploration and Edwin's involvement in early colonial projects. The first entry is for eight volumes in Chinese, and there are also works on the 'East Indies'. Oxford, Bodleian Library, Library Records b. 903, p. 155.

Domina
KATHARINA SANDYS
VXOR *Edwini Sandys*
DE LONDON MILI-
TIS, DONAVIT. XX.
LIBRAS QVIBVS EM
PTI SVNT LIB.
SEQVEN
TES.

Octo volumina Lingua Chinensi. f.

Vlysses Aldrovandus de reliquis animalibus
exanguibus. f. Bon. 1606.

Leon. Lessius de Iustitia & Iure. f.
Par. 1606.

Annib. Scoti Comment. in Scotum. f. Ro. 1589

Photij Bibliotheca Lat. cum Scholijs f.
Aug. Vind. 1606.

Dan. Tossanus in tres Evangelistas. Mat.
Luc. Io. 4. Han.

Obeliscus Vaticanus Sixti. v. Pontificis. 4.
Ro. 1587.

Salustij Opera ex recognitione Gruteri. 8.
Franc. 1607.

Zoroastri Tenelli Medicæ Consultationes.

4. Sen. 1605.

Histoire vniverselle des Indes Orient. & Oci-
dent. per Witefliet. & Ant. M. f. Dovai. 1605.

India Orient. pars 7ª autore Gerardo Artbus.
1606.

Casp. Bauhini Theatrum Anatomicum. 8.
Franc. 1605.

Io. Passerotij Orationes. & Præfationes. Idem
de Literarum inter se cognatione. Ejusdem Ka-
lenda Ianuaria. Ejusdem Oeuures Poetiques
8. Par. 1605.

Rod. Gualteri Archetypi Homiliarum. in
Lucam. 8. Tig. 1605.

Wen. Arnisæi Doctrina Politica 4. Franc. 1606.

Indagatio definitionis Logicæ Hor. Cornachini
4. Par. 1605.

Il Mundo Magico di Cesare della Riviera. 4.
Mil. 1605.

Gio. Nic. Doglioni del Theatro Vniuersale
de Prencipi. 2. vol. 4. Ven. 1606.

Iac. Lectij Editio Poetarum. Græc. veterum.
f. Aur. 1606.

Hispaniæ illustratæ To. 3. f. Franc. 1606.

Eusebij Pamphili Thesaurus temporum cum
Castigat. & notis Ios. Scaligeri f. Lugd.

Florilegium Philosophicum. Abrahami de

Exchequer official who was also an avid book collector, recorded his gifts from others, and especially noted titles that came from an author – for example, the playwright John Heywood, whose *Workes* he labels 'liber Ric. Stonley. ex dono Johannis Heywood'. It was important to him to record his own possession of the texts, but also demonstrate that they connected him with his friends and interests.[65]

Gifts and politics: the seventeenth century

Two of the books given to Thomas Bodley for his developing library at Oxford were Francis Bacon's scientific writings, *The Advancement of Learning* (1605) and *Novum Organum* (1620) (figure 4.13). The former was offered by the author to the Bodleian's founder 'in regard of your great and rare desert of learning' since he had 'built an Ark to save learning from deluge'.[66] Bacon inherited the ideals of an international community of the learned from Erasmus and other earlier humanists. By the early seventeenth century this had come to be described as a European-wide 'republic of letters'. However, he was also enmeshed in the pursuit of political patronage, struggling for preferment in a court that had become more competitive as Elizabeth I aged, and war and adverse economic circumstances curtailed royal largesse. When Bacon wrote the first version of his famous *Essays*, published in 1597, he praised learning unequivocally, but also displayed a pragmatic awareness about politics informed by Roman stoic thought (with more than a nod to Machiavelli). The *Essays* in both this first edition and the enlarged second one of 1612 still adhered to the idea of his circle as bonded through learning. In 1597 he dedicated them to his 'loving and beloved' brother Anthony. In 1612 his text was intended for James I's oldest son, Prince Henry, the future hope of the Jacobean court. When Henry tragically died in that year, Bacon opted instead for his brother-in-law and old friend Sir John Constable, whose society he valued for 'straight friendship and society, and particularly of communication in studies'.[67]

In the last expansion of the *Essays*, published in 1625, the dedicatee could not have been a greater contrast. The royal favourite, and Bacon's previous patron, George Villiers, duke of Buckingham, was offered the gift of 'the best fruits' of Bacon's labours. The gift was enhanced by having a beautifully embroidered copy made, with Villiers' image on both covers (figure 4.14). The confident language of the dedication conceals that this was a blatant appeal for favour. Between the second and third versions Bacon's rise to the

4.13 Francis Bacon's *Novum Organum* (1620), in which he proposed a new system of logic, now often termed the Baconian method, which was very influential on scientific practice. Bacon's personal badge of the wild boar is embroidered on the purple velvet cover. This copy was given to the Bodleian by the author. Oxford, Bodleian Library, Arch. A c.5, lower cover.

Lord Chancellorship had been meteoric and his fall in 1621 cataclysmic. Accused of corruption in how he dispensed justice, he was impeached by Parliament, removed from office and heavily fined. Buckingham, already at risk of parliamentary attack himself, failed to defend him, and there was no way back from the disgrace. And Bacon had been his own worst enemy. While in his celebrated *Essays* he pronounced on the virtues of impartial justice – 'above all things, integrity is the portion and proper virtue [of a judge]' – he failed to heed his own advice. His warnings to his readers not only to 'bind thine own hands or thy servants' hands from taking but bind also the hands of suitors from offering' was admirable in theory, but less easy to achieve in practice.[68]

Bacon's own observations in the *Essays* tell us much about the nature of politics in the Jacobean court. The achievement of power, he notes, is 'by a winding stair; and if there be factions, it is good to side a man's self whilst he is in the rising'. In 'Of Followers and Friends' he argues that great men must take good advice, seeking mutual support from loyal dependants, yet there is little true friendship in the world 'and least of all between equals'. In 'Of Seditions and Troubles' he even dares to invoke the dangerous writing of Machiavelli: 'as Machiavel noteth well, when princes, who ought to be common parents, make themselves a party, and lean to a side, it is as a boat that is overthrown by uneven weight.'[69] While Bacon sought to articulate general truths about political behaviour, his comments seem to map onto James I's court more easily than that of his predecessor. In some ways James I presided over a political system that was more open and generous than that of Elizabeth. When he arrived in England he saw his new state as flowing with milk and honey and rewarded his courtiers and the wider political elites freely. When the Three Graces danced before the king at a Christmas masque in 1603 they celebrated 'Desert, Reward and Gratitude'. James was profligate in these early years, handing out honours, money and jewels with little heed for the consequences.

Within a few years of James's arrival in England the royal favourites, first Robert Carr, earl of Somerset, and then George Villiers, duke of Buckingham, had established formidable control over patronage and much of the Crown's largesse flowed through their hands. The consequence was thought to be an increase in corruption: benefits and gifts were given a market price. When, for example, the earl of Suffolk was offered a New Year's gift of £500 by those who collected the royal customs taxes (over

4.14 Francis Bacon's *Essays* (1625), his final version of this popular work. This copy was presented to George Villiers, duke of Buckingham, one of the most influential men in England. Bacon had the duke's portrait embroidered on the upper and lower covers. Oxford, Bodleian Library, Arch. G e.36, upper cover.

clineth to Contention, Enmity, and War : Because the way of one
Competitor, to the attaining of his desire, is to kill, subdue, supplant,
or repell the other. Particularly, competition of praise, enclineth
to a reverence of Antiquity. For men contend with the living, not
with the dead ; to these ascribing more than due, that they may ob-
scure the glory of the other.

Civil obedi-
ence from
love of Ease.
    Desire of Ease, and sensuall Delight, disposeth men to obey a com-
mon Power : Because by such Desires, a man doth abandon the protection might be hoped for from his own Industry, and labour. Fear

From feare
of Death, or
Wounds.
of Death, and Wounds, disposeth to the same; and for the same reason.
On the contrary, needy men, and hardy, not contented with their
present condition ; as also, all men that are ambitious of Military
command, are enclined to continue the causes of warre ; and to
stirre up trouble and sedition : for there is no honour Military but by
warre ; nor any such hope to mend an ill game, as by causing a new
shuffle.

And from
love of Arts.
    Desire of Knowledge, and Arts of Peace, enclineth men to obey a
common Power : For such Desire, containeth a desire of leasure ; and
consequently protection from some other Power than their own.

Love of Ver-
tue, from love
of Praise.
    Desire of Praise, disposeth to laudable actions, such as please them
whose judgement they value ; for of those men whom we contemn,
we contemn also the Praises. Desire of Fame after death does the
same. And though after death, there be no sense of the praise given
us on Earth, as being joyes, that are either swallowed up in the unspeakable joyes of Heaven, or extinguished in the extreme torments
of Hell : yet is not such Fame vain ; because men have a present delight therein, from the foresight of it, and of the benefit that may re-
dound thereby to their posterity : which though they now see not, yet
they imagine ; and any thing that is pleasure in the sense, the same also
is pleasure in the imagination.

Hate, from
difficulty of
Requiting
great Bene-
fits.
    To have received from one, to whom we think our selves equall,
greater benefits than there is hope to Requite, disposeth to counterfeit
love ; but really secret hatred ; and puts a man into the estate of a desperate debtor, that in declining the sight of his creditor, tacitly wi-
shes him there, where he might never see him more. For benefits oblige ; and obligation is thraldome ; and unrequitable obligation,
perpetuall thraldome ; which is to ones equall, hatefull. But to have
received benefits from one, whom we acknowledge for superiour,
enclines to love ; because the obligation is no new depression : and
cheerfull acceptation, (which men call *Gratitude*,) is such an honour
done to the obliger, as is taken generally for retribution. Also to receive benefits, though from an equall, or inferiour, as long as there is
hope of requitall, disposeth to love : for in the intention of the receiver, the obligation is of ayd, and service mutuall ; from whence pro-
ceedeth an Emulation of who shall exceed in benefiting ; the most
noble and profitable contention possible ; wherein the victor is pleased with his victory, and the other revenged by confessing it.

And from
Conscience of
deserving to
be hated.
    To have done more hurt to a man, than he can, or is willing to ex-
piate, enclineth the doer to hate the sufferer. For he must expect revenge,

£60,000 in today's values), they were told bluntly that it was not enough. The going rate turned out to be £1,500. By the beginning of the 1620s opponents of the favourites brought charges of corruption in Parliament. The attack on Bacon was followed by one on Sir Lionel Cranfield, the lord treasurer, and finally in 1626 by the impeachment of Buckingham himself. Only after the latter's assassination in 1628 did Charles I reassert a stronger royal control over gift-giving, intending to make the Crown the focus of patronage again.[70]

The gift continued to be thought a burden as well as a benefit to both giver and receiver. As the Isle of Wight gentleman Sir John Oglander put it in 1622: 'if any man should think to engage me by his gifts, I would regive him twice as much again, and thereby make myself a freeman.'[71] It was the great philosopher Thomas Hobbes (1588–1679) who later shone a cold analytical light on difficulty created by a social system bonded by gifts and favours (figure 4.15). Hobbes argued in *Leviathan* (1651) that men could only be bound by the contract which they chose freely to enter, surrendering their natural rights to a sovereign in order to secure peace and self-preservation. The gift, and other forms of mutual exchange, could not have the imperative force of the contract. This did not mean that social transactions of this kind were insignificant. Gifts between equals could breed hatred rather than love: above all 'benefits oblige, and obligation is thraldome; and unrequitable obligation perpetuall thraldome'. In theory the market, with its rational calculation of interest, freed an individual from these entwined relationships so characteristic of early modern society. Yet neither Hobbes nor that later exponent of the power of the market Adam Smith necessarily thought that it was wise to abandon the interpersonal connections articulated through the gift. Smith, in *The Theory of Moral Sentiments* (1759), argued strongly for the utilization of forms of exchange that upheld status and regard. Hobbes, echoing Seneca, urged that 'a man which receiveth Benefit from another of mere Grace, [should] Endeavour that he which giveth it, have no reasonable cause to repent him of his good will.'[72] Hobbes and Smith theorized about a new form of society; nevertheless they recognized the worth of the bonds of friendship, generosity, honour and trust in sustaining what has been called 'the economy of regard'. Whether through authors' dedications, books themselves, money, food and other presents or favours, at every level of society the gift remained a principal channel through which such regard could be expressed.[73]

4.15 In *Leviathan* (1651), his influential treatise on social structures and forms of government, Thomas Hobbes reflects on how gifts and the obligations they impose can sometimes lead to hatred, sometimes to love or loyalty. Oxford, Bodleian Library, Vet. A3 c.241, p. 48.

There is always light behind the clouds

Little
Women

Louisa
May Alcott

Jo happened to suit Aunt March, who was lame and
childless old lady had offered to adopt one of the gir
because her offer was declined. Other friends told t
embered in the rich old lady's will, but the unw

can't give up our girls for a dozen fortunes. Ri
her."

old lady wouldn't speak to them for a time, bu
cal face and blunt manners struck the old lady'
did not suit Jo at all, but she accepted the plac
ise, go
hed ho
er to co
eppery

ect that
e Marc

"
I LIKE GOOD
STRONG WORDS
THAT MEAN
SOMETHING

"

- *Louisa May Alcott*

Chapter 5

The Gift of Reading

Faith Binckes

'"Christmas won't be Christmas without any presents," grumbled Jo, lying on the rug.' So opens Louisa May Alcott's classic *Little Women; or Meg, Jo, Beth and Amy*. In the opening chapters we witness the March sisters struggling with their circumstances, as a family of mid-nineteenth-century girls without money or a male breadwinner. But all is not lost, as on Christmas morning Jo does find a present, a 'crimson-covered book', under her pillow:

> She woke Meg with a 'Merry Christmas,' and bade her see
> what was under her pillow. A green-covered book appeared,
> with the same picture inside, and a few words written by
> their mother, which made their one present very precious
> in their eyes. Presently Beth and Amy woke to rummage
> and find their little books also, one dove-colored, the other
> blue, and all sat looking at and talking about them, while
> the east grew rosy with the coming day.[74]

One after the other, each sister is reminded that she already has what is important. The distinctive yet related books remind them that they are part of a family. Jo's book tells 'that beautiful old story of the best life ever lived', a reminder of the true significance of Christmas, and of the sisters' membership of a community of belief. This is reinforced by the 'few words written by their mother', which instruct her daughters to 'read and love and mind these books'. Like the rest of the novel, the Christmas book-giving ritual is rooted in a particular historical time and place. But, as the multiple reinventions of *Little Women* show, Alcott's story of sisterhood, female resilience and creativity continues to be relevant. So does the ritual. This is demonstrated by a gift box from 2022 (figure 5.1) which foregrounds Jo's defence of her outspokenness – '"I like good strong words that mean something"' – in a message of empowerment suitable for a twenty-first-century audience.[75]

5.1 Contemporary gift pack based on Louisa May Alcott, *Little Women*. Alcott's themes of sisterhood, creativity and resilience have made her novel a popular gift item. Literary Emporium, *Little Women* gift set. Image © Literary Emporium, Frome, Somerset: www.literaryemporium.co.uk.

Mr Fezziwigs Ball.

London, Chapman & Hall, 186, Strand.

A CHRISTMAS CAROL

IN PROSE.

BEING

A Ghost Story of Christmas.

BY

CHARLES DICKENS.

WITH ILLUSTRATIONS BY JOHN LEECH.

LONDON:

CHAPMAN & HALL, 186, STRAND.

MDCCCXLIII.

This chapter focuses largely on examples from the nineteenth and twentieth centuries, periods of innovation in the relationship between the gift and the book. Marcel Mauss argued for the gift as an unavoidably social phenomenon, which represented and mediated the world that had produced it.[76] And so this was a relationship that also expressed the animating social and political challenges of the times – whether they were war, issues of racial justice or the role of women. Just as Alcott made sure that there was a sharp edge to her Christmas scene, the writers and artists we will focus on explored the gift as a site of ambivalence or tension – a struggle that can be registered in the form of the book, in the way the gift is represented in or by the book, or in both.

Christmas gift-books: on the line between darkness and light

When we consider the gift via this combination of literary innovation, commercial savvy and social conscience, Charles Dickens is one of the first figures to come to mind. As Patrick Scott observes, 'the paradox and the genius of Dickens's Christmas books is that, while they were *about* giving, they were at the same time designed to *be* gifts.'[77] He argues that Dickens combined the established yet waning popularity of the literary annual with the emerging genre of the dedicated Christmas gift-book. The latter were illustrated anthologies, bound 'in brilliant reds, blues, and greens picked out with gilt, [which] announced their exchange value as gifts to be presented and displayed'.[78] The transitional form of the first edition of *A Christmas Carol* is appropriate given its interest in balance – the line between self and others, misery and joy, past and future. At its heart is Ebenezer Scrooge, a character so unacquainted with Christmas spirit that Dickens arranged several personal introductions.

A Christmas Carol in prose, being a Ghost Story of Christmas was first published in London in 1843, during a period of famine and economic depression. In response, Dickens emphasized responsibility and community, along with those bonds forged through the happiness of bringing happiness to others. One of the most engaging examples of this is the ball held by Scrooge's first employer Mr Fezziwig, which Scrooge revisits with the Ghost of Christmas Past. Fezziwig fizzes with brio and good humour. He opens his house, heart and wallet while remaining very much the master of the scene. This is captured in John Leech's colour illustration on the frontispiece to the first edition (figure 5.2). Fezziwig occupies centre

previous pages **5.2** John Leech's frontispiece illustration to the first edition of *A Christmas Carol* emphasizes the ideal of community and bountiful giving through the figure of Mr Fezziwig. Oxford, Bodleian Library, 43.230, frontispiece and title page.

opposite **5.3** 'The air was filled with phantoms': Arthur Rackham's illustrations for the 1915 edition of *A Christmas Carol* emphasize the spectral, disturbing quality of Dickens's ghost story. Oxford, Bodleian Library, Castello 371, facing page 32.

stage, poised but in motion, beneath a bunch of vibrant Christmas greenery. His wife looks on affectionately. And so do we readers, anticipating a book that is similarly controlled yet dynamic, able to balance on tiptoe between darkness and light. After all, we are reading a 'Ghost Story', a Christmas tradition that is pleasurably familiar, but retains its power to chill. Dickens never lets us forget that suffering is as communicable as delight. 'Remove me!' Scrooge pleads with the Spirit more than once, 'I cannot bear it!'[79]

The immediate success of *A Christmas Carol* was enduring, and, although the Christmas gift-book would fall out of favour, the market for high-quality illustrated books suitable for giving remained strong. William Heinemann and J.B. Lippincott's lavish 1915 edition of *A Christmas Carol* is a good example. It contained images by one of Britain's most celebrated illustrators: Arthur Rackham. The Bodleian's copy is part of a signed, limited *edition de luxe*, which framed the gift-book as artwork and as investment. As an object, this volume gives an entirely different impression from Dickens's first edition. Equally striking is the difference between the visual styles of Rackham and Leech. Rackham's sinuous lines and watery tones never lose their otherworldliness, even when depicting the homely Fezziwig ball. In Rackham's version, Mr and Mrs Fezziwig emerge from an abstract background, two figures on a deserted stage. In the preceding illustration (figure 5.3), 'phantoms' crowd the frame, pushing Scrooge into the top right-hand corner. Rackham's style had been forged long before the outbreak of the First World War, but we can wonder what this scene of bustling, wailing ghosts might have meant to contemporary readers. As Lucy Shaw notes, in the following year Rackham illustrated *The Allies' Fairy Book*, part of a trend that saw gift-books sold in support of the war effort.[80] These two editions of *A Christmas Carol* help us to compare and contrast two periods of crisis and transition, both in the form of the book and in the wider world in which those books appeared.

War also marks the entrance of a character as celebrated as Scrooge, albeit one whose association with the Christmas season is less obvious. 'John H. Watson, M.D.' has been invalided out of conflict in Afghanistan, and his search for an inexpensive London flatshare leads him to a certain Sherlock Holmes. When Watson happens across Holmes's theory of the 'Science of Deduction and Analysis' in a magazine, he jokingly compares him with existing fictional detectives. Holmes is far from flattered, dismissing even Edgar Allan Poe's famous sleuth Dupin as 'showy and

5.4 The cover of *Beeton's Christmas Annual* for 1887 shows an illustration by D.H. Friston in striking colour. 'A Study in Scarlet' is the first published appearance of Sherlock Holmes, and this issue is now a rare and valuable item. Oxford, Bodleian Library, Arch. AA e.155 (1887), upper cover.

28 1887

PRICE ONE SHILLING.

BEETON'S·CHRISTMAS·ANNUAL

A STUDY IN SCARLET

By A. CONAN DOYLE

Containing · also
Two Original
DRAWING ROOM PLAYS.
I.
FOOD FOR POWDER.
By R. ANDRE
2
THE FOUR LEAVED SHAMROCK
By C. J. HAMILTON

With ENGRAVINGS
By D. H. FRISTON
MATT STRETCH,
AND
R. ANDRÉ

WARD·LOCK·&·CO
LONDON·NEW·YORK
AND·MELBOURNE.

superficial'.[81] Before long we will have the chance to judge for ourselves, as Holmes and Watson embark on a case. The first outing of this iconic pair was titled 'A Study in Scarlet' and it took place in 1887 on the pages of *Beeton's Christmas Annual*. What is now one of the most valuable magazine issues in the world was then a popular, one-shilling publication, in which Conan Doyle appeared alongside a couple of parlour plays. The combination of death and festive family fun – comparable with the tradition of the Christmas ghost story – was suggested by the cover image (figure 5.4). It is saturated with crimson, echoing both the season and the 'scarlet thread of murder' informing the story's title.[82] Despite Holmes's dislike of showiness, 'A Study in Scarlet' was as highly coloured as the cover. The mystery even hinged on two of the central themes of melodrama: the separation of true lovers and the perils of forced marriage. The giving of women in matrimony – and the abuse that could accompany that tradition of the gift – is represented from the early stages of the story by a wedding ring found near one of the slain men. Holmes recognizes the ring as a key piece of evidence, as it becomes clear that this is a tale of revenge, in which the murder victims are far from innocent.

Women, gifts and other dangerous things

However, although she is crucial to the plot, the avenged woman in 'A Study in Scarlet' remains more or less a stock figure. She appears first as a golden-haired child, and then as a virtuous young woman, who conveniently dies of a broken heart. In other words, she plays to the stereotype of the literary annual as a venue for lightweight reading matter aimed at an undemanding, often female, audience. This was even more true for the highly popular gift-books that proliferated in the earlier decades of the nineteenth century, pioneered by Rudolph Ackermann and his first title, *Forget Me Not*. In her introduction to *The Annual, being a selection from the Forget-Me-Nots, Keepsakes, and other Annuals of the Nineteenth Century*, Vita Sackville-West ponders the genre with an eyebrow firmly raised: 'What more suitable present for a gentleman to give a lady? Or a nephew, anxiously hunting for a Christmas present for his aunt? One of the minor problems of life was solved.'[83]

More recent scholarship has uncovered a different side to these publications.[84] As Christine Alexander and Jane Sellars have shown, the young Charlotte Brontë was a keen reader of literary annuals, using them as inspiration for her own early writing and artwork. When we view the genre through the lens supplied by the Brontës, it is harder to dismiss readers as passive consumers of romance and moral instruction. Charlotte turned to the 1831 number of *Forget Me Not* more than once, converting its monochrome illustration of the story 'Bessy Bell and Mary Gray. A Scottish Legend of 1666' (figure 5.5) into a coloured image of her own (figure 5.6). She gave Bessy and Mary the identifying features of the story, enlivening the more generic figures of the engraving. She brightened the scene throughout, lightening both sky and landscape, and adding pink blossoms to match Bessy's dress. But the easy, close embrace of the two best friends – which is at the heart of the plot and of the famous Scottish ballad on which it was based – remained unaltered.

This version of the tale explored female friendship and romantic competition, as Bessy falls in love with the young man to whom Mary is secretly engaged. The happiness of one will mean the unhappiness of the other, or so it seems, until Mary's fiancé decides to give her a necklace as a keepsake while he is overseas. This gift will be fatal to both women, as it carries the plague. Bessy falls ill while nursing her friend, and they die and are buried together. This tainted gift is a powerful but ambiguous device. Like the wedding ring in 'A Study in Scarlet', the necklace reminds us that marriage is linked with transaction. Valuable and beautiful things – jewellery, women – change hands, with the expectation that the less tangible bonds of friendship will be set aside. But here the vehicle designed to cement this process becomes the mechanism that prevents it. Bessy and Mary remain together in death as they were in life, even surviving into legend as a byword for sisterly fidelity and courage.

Brontë enjoyed working on the melancholy, late-Romantic scenes that appeared in these gift-books. Nonetheless, her focus on the vivacity of Bessy and Mary hinted that female potential was defined neither by men nor by marriage. Such bonds are central to Jill Rappoport's work on women and gifts in the Victorian period. She argues that although women operated as or like gifts within a male-dominated world, they could also use gifts to forge and to manage networks of alliance.[85] This was a complex, delicate business, reflected in the language women used to frame acts of giving and receiving. We can see this in Brontë's response to her publisher George Smith, on receipt of a package of books from him in 1848. She gleefully sprang open one of the secret mechanisms of the gift, acknowledging that gratitude – 'the infliction of thanks' – could be a mixed blessing:

5.5 An illustration for the story 'Bessy Bell and Mary Gray. A Scottish Legend of 1666', from the gift annual *Forget Me Not*, 1831 (published late 1830). Such collections of stories, poems, essays and illustrations were a popular gift at this time. Oxford, Bodleian Library, Johnson f.996, facing p. 361.

5.6 Watercolour by Charlotte Brontë, 'Bessy Bell and Mary Gray' (December 1830), based on the illustration from *Forget Me Not*. The teenaged Brontë sisters were enthusiastic readers of gift-books, and Charlotte transformed their romantic scenarios and dilemmas in her own complex fiction. © The Brontë Society, C 11: 5.6

if you are overwhelmed, I am sorry, but I cannot help it,
nor can I diminish one atom of the burden. The case for me
stands as it did before; it was not so much by the sacrifice
your gifts cost you that I reckoned their value, as by the
pleasure they gave me, and as that pleasure is enhanced
by what you tell me, I ought to be, and, I hope, am, still
more grateful.[86]

Here, Brontë asserts her dominance as a recipient, through her ability to
determine the value of what she has been given regardless of the intentions
of the (well-connected, male) giver. In contrast, when Brontë's contemporary
Elizabeth Gaskell received Anna Jameson's *A Commonplace Book of Thoughts*
from its author in 1854, this was her gloriously overripe response:

Here is the beautiful Commonplace book awaiting me on
my return home! And I give it a great welcome you may be
sure; and turn it over, & peep in, and read a sentence and
shut it up to think over its graceful suggestive wisdom in
something of the 'gourmet' spirit of a child with an eatable
dainty; which child, if it have the proper artistic sensuality
of childhood, first looks its cake over to appreciate the full
promise of its appearance, – next, snuffs up its fragrance,
– and gets to a fair & complete mouth-watering before it
plunges into the first bite.[87]

Commonplace books gathered brief, memorable sections of prose and
poetry. By comparing herself to a greedy yet innocent child peeping in at
these 'graceful' little mouthfuls, Gaskell managed both to express and to
distance herself from 'proper artistic sensuality'. The literary content of
these gifts seemed to interest the women less than the opportunity they
presented for articulations of female authority and female pleasure.

The difficult, even dangerous, relationship between pleasure and
exchange is central to one of the most famous poems by a woman writer
of the next generation: Christina Rossetti's 'Goblin Market', published
first in 1862.[88] It is the story of two sisters – Laura and Lizzie – who are as
close as Bessy Bell and Mary Gray. Despite Lizzie's warnings about the
magical 'goblin market' and its alluring wares, Laura gives in to temptation.
Without any money, she exchanges a lock of her golden hair for some of the
delicious 'eatables' on offer. Disaster ensues, and she can only be saved by

5.7 Christina Rossetti's poem 'Goblin
Market' explores both the dangers and
the power of exchange and sacrifice
through the story of the sisters Lizzie and
Laura. This illustration for the first edition
of 1862 is by Christina's brother and
celebrated artist, Dante Gabriel Rossetti.
Oxford, Bodleian Library, (OC) 280 k.221,
frontispiece.

MMF & Co.

Lizzie, who braves the rage of the 'goblin men' as they try unsuccessfully to force her to do the same. With a 'silver penny' to exchange instead, Lizzie runs home bruised but victorious, and Laura is restored by a taste of some of the fruit that has been smeared on her sister during the struggle. Even this brief outline indicates why the poem has been so irresistible to readers, illustrators and critics alike. Rossetti blended biblical and fairy-tale tropes, female agency and community, consumer and erotic desire, with an awareness that women were subject to market forces by turns enchanting and brutal. The first illustrator of *Goblin Market and Other Poems* was Rossetti's brother, the artist and poet Dante Gabriel Rossetti, whose depiction of the two sisters placed them within the iconography of the Pre-Raphaelite muse (figure 5.7). This sumptuous interpretation highlighted a central problem. Rossetti's poem about the gift of sisterly solidarity had become an alluring object within a marketplace, and its central female characters objects to be consumed. The gorgeous book radiates 'proper artistic sensuality', but how does this relate to Laura, whose sensuality leads her into terrible danger?

'An object amongst other objects': gifts, books and abolition

The sense that this book both warns against and participates in a form of objectification points us towards a far more disturbing aspect of women's role in the nineteenth-century gift economy. At the time when Gaskell, Brontë and Rossetti were writing, chattel slavery was still practised in North America. Recent research by Stephanie E. Jones-Rogers has revealed the extent of women's ownership of enslaved people, a practice facilitated by inheritance and by gift-giving.[89] This is exactly what is described in the opening pages of William and Ellen Craft's extraordinary autobiography *Running a Thousand Miles for Freedom: Or, the Escape of William and Ellen Craft from Slavery*:

> My wife's first master was her father, and her mother his slave, and the latter is still the slave of his widow. Notwithstanding my wife being of African extraction on her mother's side, she is almost white – in fact, she is so nearly so that the tyrannical old lady to whom she first belonged became so annoyed, at finding her frequently mistaken for a child of the family, that she gave her when eleven years of age to a daughter, as a wedding present.[90]

This depiction of a person with the legal status of an object is all the more devastating for being so matter-of-fact. Ellen's biological father was her 'first master'. We can assume that the 'tyrannical old lady to whom she first belonged' was his wife, who separated Ellen from her mother and passed her down the family line. The reason – that Ellen was 'frequently mistaken for a child of the family' – is hardly surprising, given that Ellen *was* 'a child of the family'. The real mistake lay with a system built on absurdity as well as atrocity, which ripped apart the bonds of sisterhood we have seen so carefully woven in the examples above.

This verbal image of Ellen as 'wedding present' is preceded by an equally startling, but entirely different, image on the frontispiece (figure 5.8). At first sight it seems to show a well-dressed young gentleman in shaded glasses, with a direct gaze and a bandaged arm. But underneath, the caption reads 'Ellen Craft: the fugitive slave'. At Christmas in 1848, the Crafts used Ellen's light skin as part of an audacious disguise that allowed them to escape from Georgia to Philadelphia and freedom. In order to travel together, Ellen posed as an injured White man, and William as 'his' attendant. The bandaged arm was to prevent Ellen from having to sign her assumed name, as in Georgia slaves were kept illiterate. The glasses concealed her eyes, and Christmas was selected as a few days of holiday were likely to be granted, giving them a head start. In this way, the couple journeyed across the Southern states in plain sight, improvising their performance as they went, defying the terrifying consequences of discovery. Ellen's successful crossing of the boundaries of geography, sex, race and class turned slavery's investment in mistaken identities – not least the wilful mistaking of persons for things – against it.

Running a Thousand Miles for Freedom was published in London, as the Fugitive Slave Act of 1850 made it too risky for the Crafts to remain in America. The book joined a long-established canon of abolitionist literature, in which formerly enslaved people related the unspeakable, and charted their progress towards emancipation. One of the earliest examples is *The Interesting Narrative of the Life of Olaudah Equiano, or Gustavus Vassa, the African: Written by Himself* (figure 5.9). By the time it appeared in 1789, Equiano had already published letters in London newspapers, speaking out against the horrors of the slave trade from the perspective of one who had endured them. Equiano understood the significance and the nuance of his authorship.[91] Not only did he maintain

ELLEN CRAFT.

RUNNING A THOUSAND MILES

FOR FREEDOM;

OR, THE ESCAPE

OF

WILLIAM AND ELLEN CRAFT

FROM SLAVERY.

" Slaves cannot breathe in England : if their lungs
Receive our air, that moment they are free ;
They touch our country, and their shackles fall."

COWPER.

LONDON:
WILLIAM TWEEDIE, 337, STRAND.

1860.

210. m. 110.

5.8 This frontispiece portrait of Ellen
Craft presents her passing as an ailing
White gentleman: part of her audacious
plan with her husband William to liberate
themselves from enslavement in Georgia,
in the southern United States. Oxford,
Bodleian Library, (OC) 210 m.110, title page
opening.

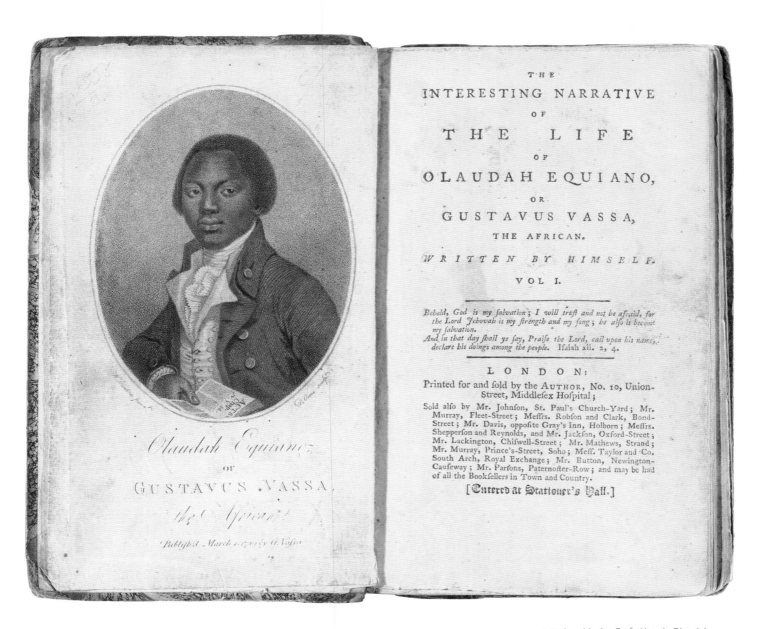

THE

INTERESTING NARRATIVE

OF

THE LIFE

OF

OLAUDAH EQUIANO,

OR

GUSTAVUS VASSA,

THE AFRICAN.

WRITTEN BY HIMSELF.

VOL I.

Behold, God is my salvation; I will trust and not be afraid, for the Lord Jehovah is my strength and my song; he also is become my salvation.
And in that day shall ye say, Praise the Lord, call upon his name, declare his doings among the people. Isaiah xii. 2, 4.

LONDON:

Printed for and sold by the AUTHOR, No. 10, Union-Street, Middlesex Hospital;

Sold also by Mr. Johnson, St. Paul's Church-Yard; Mr. Murray, Fleet-Street; Messrs. Robson and Clark, Bond-Street; Mr. Davis, opposite Gray's Inn, Holborn; Messrs. Shepperson and Reynolds, and Mr. Jackson, Oxford-Street; Mr. Lackington, Chiswell-Street; Mr. Mathews, Strand; Mr. Murray, Prince's-Street, Soho; Mess. Taylor and Co. South Arch, Royal Exchange; Mr. Button, Newington-Causeway; Mr. Parsons, Paternoster-Row; and may be had of all the Booksellers in Town and Country.

[Entered at Stationer's Hall.]

Olaudah Equiano,

OR

GUSTAVUS VASSA,

the African.

Published March 1789 by G. Vassa

5.9 As with the Crafts' book, Olaudah Equiano's *The Interesting Narrative …* (1789) frames its author with great care, as Equiano's composure and self-possession stand alongside various, differing markers of his identity, and the book's full title stresses the authenticity of his account. Oxford, Bodleian Library, Vet. A5 f.3496/1, title page opening.

the copyright and market the book himself, but every aspect of his visual representation added weight to his argument for abolition. His expression is modest yet composed, he holds a Bible, and he is dressed as a fashionable English gentleman.

Equiano's ownership of his story, his image and both his names emerge from a backdrop cross-hatched with possession and exchange. At the opening of *The Interesting Narrative* he outlines how gifts and property operate within his home culture (in what is now southern Nigeria). We learn that brides become the property of their husband, and that 'slaves' can form part of her dowry.[92] After his capture, aged around eleven, Equiano finds himself thrown into an annihilating, industrial-scale version of this bondage. Having survived the Middle Passage, his name is changed more than once, as he is passed from one captor to another. At one point a ship's captain named Pascal purchases him 'as a present for some … friends in England'.[93] But he also receives gifts – including gifts of books. Spiritual and material rewards are united in Chapter IV, on the day of his baptism:

> [S]o I was baptized in St. Margaret's church, Westminster, in February 1759, by my present name. The clergyman, at the same time, gave me a book, called a Guide to the Indians, written by the Bishop of Sodor and Man. On this occasion Miss Guerin did me the honour to stand as godmother, and afterwards gave me a treat.[94]

The clergyman's gift was likely to have been Thomas Wilson's *The Knowledge and Practice of Christianity Made Easy to the Meanest Capacities: Or, an Essay Towards an Instruction for the Indians.* This popular catechism had originally been intended for the Muscogee Nation, who in the 1730s and 1740s were still living on their ancestral lands in Alabama and Georgia. In an Author's Preface aimed at fellow members of missionary societies, Wilson partially excused the transatlantic slave trade, on condition that slavers and plantation owners encouraged conversion to Christianity and permitted religious observance by enslaved people. Without this, Wilson sternly noted, 'it will be very difficult to justify *the Trade of* BUYING, TRANSPORTING, *and* SELLING *them as Beasts of Burthen.*'[95] Did Equiano receive this edition, and possibly read this justification? The Preface varied, although its sentiments towards enslavement and conversion remained similar. Either way, the gifts of book and 'treat' pull us violently in opposing directions. They were (presumably) kindly meant. But they marked steps on a religious, intellectual and legal journey crafted by the very culture that had stolen from him – that had stolen *him* – as it was still stealing others. These gifts arrive saturated with appalling loss.

Abolitionists of the later eighteenth and nineteenth centuries were familiar with the depth and breadth of anti-abolitionist sentiment, which extended from uncompromisingly pro-slavery arguments to the uneasy accommodation expressed by Wilson. To counter it, they produced a battery of material in every medium available, aiming to exert political pressure, to inform the public, to win hearts and minds, and to raise funds. The gift-book, with its established appeal to sympathetic and often White, female, middle-class readers, was a useful weapon in this arsenal. Gift-books were part of a mutually supporting network of anti-slavery activities, which included newspapers, extensive public lecture tours, fairs and rallies.[96]

The most long-running abolitionist gift-book in North America was *The Liberty Bell*, which appeared between 1839 and 1858, and was timed to coincide with an annual anti-slavery bazaar in Boston.[97] The historical Liberty Bell, after which the annual was named, was symbolic of America's own struggle for independence. Slavery's affront to the biblical motto engraved on it – 'Proclaim LIBERTY Throughout all the Land unto all the Inhabitants Thereof' – thereby united opposition on both political and religious grounds. We can see the power of the Bell as an emblem in the number for 1856. In a title page illustration (figure 5.10), it hangs from a stout tree branch, above a pair of manacles still lying on the sword that has smashed them open. The image is abstract and symbolic, on the one hand, but detailed and naturalistic, on the other. This juxtaposition reminded readers that the larger spiritual, moral, political worlds coexisted within their ordinary daily lives, in the battle against slavery and in the act of reading.

The Bell also appears in the decoration at the head of Elizabeth Barrett Browning's poem 'A Curse for a Nation', which took aim not only at the moral failures of the American nation but also at corruption and poverty at home (figure 5.11). The Bell swings above the first stanza, like the prophetic voice which forces the speaker to deliver the 'curse'. Denae Dyck points to the poem's redefinition of what a curse is, and who was allowed to issue one: 'Through … rhetorical turns, the reasons that the speaker offers for her inability to write this curse – her belonging to a transatlantic family,

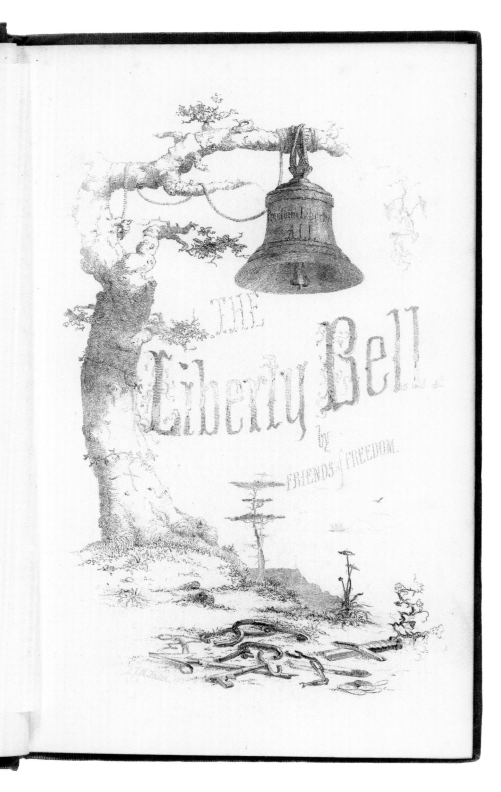

A Curse for a Nation.

BY ELIZABETH BARRETT BROWNING.

PROLOGUE.

I heard an angel speak last night,
    And he said, " Write !
Write a nation's curse for me,
And send it over the western sea."

1

her membership in a nation equally deserving of censure, and her status as a woman – become, instead, the grounds of her authority.[58] This reading reformulates the 'curse' as a type of gift. It is presented to the 'nation' with love as well as anger, as it serves up painful but necessary truths. But it is also a gift presented to the speaker, who is compelled to 'Write!' – to break her silence and to move beyond her 'proper' feminine sphere. This relationship between giving and receiving could be viewed as mutual empowerment: the struggle liberates the political voices of female abolitionists, as well as freeing the enslaved. But it also points to the position of White abolitionists as beneficiaries of the culture of enslavement they were desperate to end. The gift and the curse, once again, change places.

Your problem solved? Book tokens and the currency of giving

Perhaps – as Vita Sackville-West suggested – selecting a present is one of life's 'minor problems'. But if this chapter has shown us anything, it is that the power of a gift should not be underestimated. Even when gift-giving does not relate to issues as consequential as abolition or women's equality, the potential for anxiety is real. The prolific cataloguer of British social embarrassment, cartoonist H.M. Bateman, portrayed it in a series of images that contrasted experiences of present giving and present receiving (figure 5.12). The exaggeration may be funny, but we still recognize some element of ourselves. A man unwraps a Christmas tie, his face a picture of baffled rage. Above him, another man – perhaps the giver? – struggles to stuff a variety of parcels into the post. Opposite them stands a different couple: a woman ambling to the postbox in her furs, and a man performing a Fezziwig-style jig of delight. Even without the captions – which emphasize the 'agony' and 'risk' of the whole affair – it's clear whose example to follow. As Charlotte Brontë had done in 1848, Bateman's drawing acknowledged that gifts and gratitude could be difficult. Unlike Brontë, it also promised a way out.

The cartoon and its accompanying slogan 'YOUR PROBLEM SOLVED!' appeared on a bookmark advertising book tokens, a scheme that would soothe the 'agony' of present-choosing even more effectively than gift-books had done a century before. Book tokens first appeared in 1932, the brainchild of Harold Raymond, then director of Chatto & Windus. Raymond questioned whether all gifts truly possessed the same 'capacity for giving pleasure', arguing for a book's superiority to ordinary consumer

YOUR PROBLEM SOLVED!

Why go through all this agony?

Buy BOOK TOKENS for your friends.

No risk then of sending the wrong gift.

He can choose any book he likes.

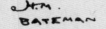

BOOK TOKENS

are on sale in bookshops and can be exchanged in any town in the British Isles for any books your friends may choose.

The Token Card costs threepence, and stamps of the following values are available: 3/6, 5/-, 7/6, 10/6, 21/-.

This bookmark is issued by the National Book Council, 3 Henrietta Street, London W.C.2

5.12 'YOUR PROBLEM SOLVED!' This early bookmark advert for book tokens, designed around a cartoon by H.M. Bateman, stresses the anxiety involved in gift-giving and the relief that the token may provide. Oxford, Bodleian Library, John Johnson Collection: Bookmarkers 5.

items such as a 'hatpin, ornament, photo frame … or ashtray'.[99] Needless to say, the benefits of this choice would also be felt by the publishing industry. The Bodleian's John Johnson Collection holds a wealth of material on the development, marketing and design of this staple of gift-giving. Framing the monetary value of the gift was vital. This involved visual branding, including images that would appear on the gift cards to which the tokens were attached, and on matching book plates. These were the items that would travel from giver to recipient, lingering within the book itself like the precious inscription of Mrs March in *Little Women*. They needed to be light and portable, on the one hand, but weighty and significant, on the other, conveying something of what a book – and reading – represented.

Hundreds of book token designs were created over the decades.[100] These were either specially commissioned, or repurposed existing paintings. Rowland Hilder, best known for his depictions of the English countryside, was one of the artists approached for bespoke designs. One bucolic scene (figure 5.13) incorporates the image of a bird carrying a book, the tokens' logo at this point. It combined this with another popular motif, of the book resting by an open window. The figures of book and bird echo one another. Together, they suggest that the gift of reading opens new horizons, transporting us intellectually and emotionally just as the token bridges the distance between giver and recipient. The ploughman and the bunch of tulips offered grounding, implying tradition, continuity and renewal. Our second example adapts an existing painting, the work of the British surrealist and official war artist John Armstrong, dating from the early 1940s (figure 5.14). The image clearly references the devastation of war, and the title is drawn from the closing lines of Shelley's 'Ode to the West Wind'. Armstrong produced variations on the same composition, not all of which carry this title.[101] While the overall message of hope and endurance remains, attaching Shelley's words did more than to make the painting appropriate for a book token by introducing literary context. 'Ode to the West Wind' was a revolutionary poem, in which destruction mingled with transformation and rebirth. And whereas spring tulips are placed politely to one side of Hilder's image, here one looms over the scene, daring us to imagine the immense possibilities of reconstruction. The final impression is elegant yet radical. It looks towards the central role new forms of art and literature might play in the making of a new society, whilst not denying the darkness and pain of recent history.

5.13 This book token was designed by celebrated landscape artist and book illustrator Rowland Hilder. The lines of text in the open book parallel the productive furrows made by the plough outside. Oxford, Bodleian Library, John Johnson Collection, Publicity Box 11.

A BOOK TOKEN

In his essay 'The Gifts of Reading', Robert MacFarlane reflects on the many ways in which the gift of books has changed his life, and the lives of others, for the better. 'The gift is kept moving', MacFarlane notes, referencing gift theorist Lewis Hyde, 'given onwards in a new form'.[102] In the model MacFarlane presents, the transformational potential of the book matches the equally transformational potential of human generosity, expanding outwards across nations, genders and generations. All the examples we have explored testify to the self-reinforcing positivity of the relationship between the gift and the book, the pleasure and power it grants, and its significance to personal and to social change. And yet positivity can only emerge in a dynamic with something else – the other faces reflected back to us in the complex process that giving represents. The gift of books allows us to explore those other perspectives too, however challenging they may be.

5.14 This book token from the 1940s, using a painting by John Armstrong, suggests that books and gifts can contribute to a creative or imaginative renewal in the midst of the ruins left by war. Oxford, Bodleian Library, John Johnson Collection, Publicity Box 11.

THIS BOOK TOKEN

is exchangeable at any Book Token bookshop in Great Britain and Ireland
for a book or books of the holder's cnoice to the value shown inside.

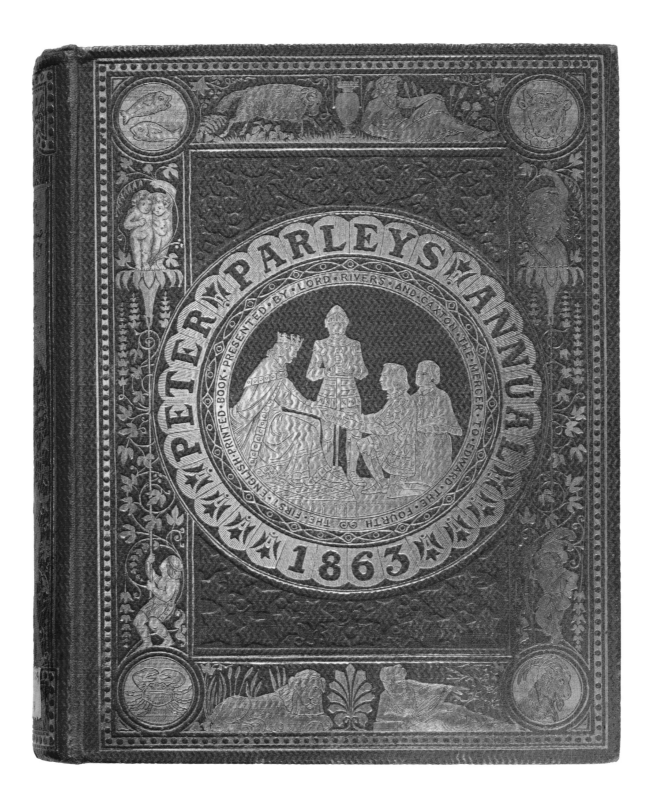

PETER PARLEY'S ANNUAL

PRESENTED BY LORD RIVERS AND CAXTON THE MERCER TO EDWARD THE FOURTH THE FIRST ENGLISH PRINTED BOOK

1863

Chapter 6

Myths of the Gift for Children and Young Adults

Maria Sachiko Cecire

Children come into the world without possessions, and so most of the things they own – including books – must be given to them, usually by adults. This is true not only for the material items that children need and want, but also for the knowledge, beliefs and stories that young people get from the adults in their lives. Children's books are tangible examples of both, as objects intended for young people to use, and also as vehicles for education and socialization. This chapter discusses beautiful gift-books and other Anglo-American works for young readers that feature generosity, inheritance and exchange. These often position myths old and new as guides that can help children lead ethical, meaningful lives. Tangled up in these ideals, however, are social expectations and biases that can exclude, demean or dehumanize some children even as they welcome others. But shifting literary contexts and the enduring importance of gifts across cultures create opportunities for lively counter-narratives that demonstrate how books and young people are well positioned to reveal, repair and reshape our imaginative and lived realities – from the reach of British royal authority and deep-rooted magic to dreams of distant galaxies.

'Instruction blended with amusement': children's gift-books and annuals

Strong feelings of affection and care are often mixed up with the inevitable power dynamic that emerges in this relationship of adult giver to child recipient in Western models of childhood. For instance, the act of giving a volume like *Peter Parley's Annual: A Christmas and New Year's Present for Young People* (figure 6.1) would have been, as holiday giving is now, a sign of the giver's fondness or at least social responsibility for the child receiving it. In the Preface to the 1832 volume of *Marshall's Christmas Box*, another long-running children's gift annual, the editor addresses his 'young friends' directly, telling readers that they will find in the book's pages 'instruction blended with amusement' – a compound goal that has

6.1 *Peter Parley's Annual* provided a mixture of stories, pictures and poems for young readers. There was a new cover design each year, this one a fanciful picture of Lord Rivers and William Caxton presenting 'the first English printed book' to King Edward IV. Oxford, Bodleian Library, Per. 2529 e.139 (1840–1885), front cover.

characterized children's literature since it emerged as a dedicated category of writing in the late eighteenth century. The editor assumes that child readers will be grateful for the book and directs their thanks for the pleasures and learning enclosed in its pages to 'his good friends and theirs': the authors and adapters of the stories.[103] This economy of giving involves multiple layers of adults who write, publish, select and purchase books for children's enjoyment and education. While these books may elicit genuine outpourings of thanks from children, they also tell us a great deal about what *adults* want and hope for the next generation.

Holiday gift-books like the *Christmas Box* were part of growing consumer markets in Britain and the United States that used the sentiments associated with gift-giving to endow increasingly affordable mass-produced books with emotional value. Books written and marketed specifically for children were still a relatively new phenomenon at the turn of the nineteenth century, as was giving Christmas gifts to children; indeed, Christmas was still only newly a child-centred holiday in the early decades of the nineteenth century.[104] But as book production technologies became cheaper over the course of industrial expansion, and as Romantic ideas about childhood as a precious, important life stage became widespread, the market began to offer more and more forms of affordable works for small hands. Over the course of the nineteenth century these included long fold-out panoramas, pop-up books, dissolving-view books, and pull-tab mechanical books for children, among other technologies of bookmaking. A volume like *A Visit to the Country* (undated; between *c.* 1875 and 1890) demonstrates the multiple ways in which young people could interact with commercial children's literature (figure 6.2).[105] That richly illustrated volume takes the form of a letter from one child to another and includes pop-up scenes from the teller's countryside adventures. The title page of the copy in the Bodleian Library's Opie Collection has been coloured in to match the cover, suggesting another creative way that a young reader chose to enjoy the text. An inscription on the inside cover notes that this book was given to 'Marjorie, from Miss Thomson' – presumably a gift to a child from an adult she knew – for 'Xmas '91'. More than just small or bowdlerized versions of adult texts, novelties like *A Visit to the Country* demonstrated that books could be designed and selected in ways that prioritize children's curiosity, interactive tendencies and desire to play.

6.2 This book is inscribed as a gift; the title page has here been coloured in to match the book's cover design, probably by its owner, Marjorie, who was given the book at Christmas 1891. Oxford, Bodleian Library, Opie EE 300, title page.

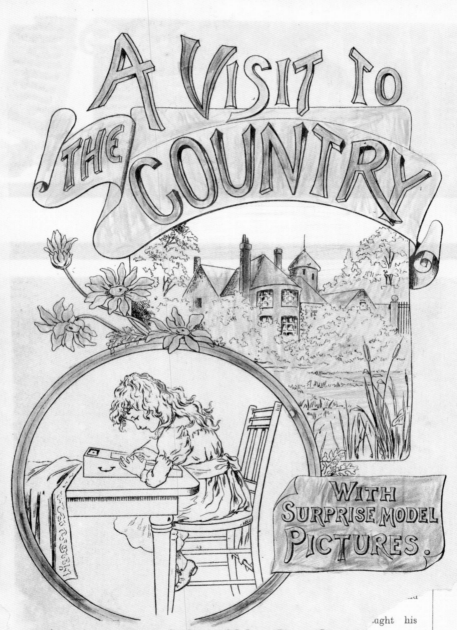

A VISIT TO THE COUNTRY

WITH SURPRISE MODEL PICTURES.

London: Dean & Son, 160a, Fleet Street

In addition to children's gift and 'toy' books like those above, series of books invited collecting in a way that hoped to create inbuilt demand for further purchases – and a straightforward plan for gifting over time, as each new instalment could be presented as it came out. Scottish writer and scholar Andrew Lang is best known today for the series of collected fairy stories that he developed and released with his wife Leonora Blanche Lang from 1889, beginning with *The Blue Fairy Book*. Like Jacob and Wilhelm Grimm in Germany, Lang was a scholar of folklore who gained widespread acclaim by publishing fairy tales for children. Unlike the Grimms, however, who had not initially intended their *Kinder- und Hausmärchen* (*Children's and Household Tales*, 1812) for specific use by children and were widely criticized for the first edition's moral unsuitability for young readers, the Langs aimed their 'Coloured' Fairy Books squarely at a child market. Published with illustrations and bound in the colour corresponding to each title, these books encouraged gift-giving and collecting. Their contents, like *Marshall's Christmas Box* and other gift-books for children, were themselves collections of stories that promised to be sources of both amusement and education.

Generosity and sacrifice in folk and fairy tales

By the nineteenth century the idea that young people learn best when enjoying themselves had begun to compete with stricter puritan ideas about education in England and the United States. Fairy tales were held up as both natural to childhood reading and vehicles of deep national identity and feeling. This association between children, mythology and the premodern past is one that remains powerful today and is perhaps one reason that adults continue to turn to folk and fairy tales as gifts for young people. Passing on these old, magical stories seems at once to honour what adults think children will enjoy, and to convey the knowledge and expectations about social life that adults hold and wish to pass on. Once fairy tales became associated with children, authors and editors were quick to adjust their contents to fit current understandings of what is 'appropriate' for young readers.

For instance, the opening tale in the Langs' *Red Fairy Book* (1890), 'The Twelve Dancing Princesses' (figure 6.3), rewrites the Grimms' version to focus on characters just at the cusp of adulthood. In Grimm, the commoner who discovers the secret of how the princesses wear out their dancing shoes every night is an old soldier; the Langs' protagonist, however, is a dreamy young cowherd-turned-garden boy named Michael. And while at the end of

6.3 In this illustration from 'The Twelve Dancing Princesses' in Andrew and Leonora Blanche Lang's *The Red Fairy Book* the young hero Michael presents flowers to Princess Lina, along with a branch he has brought back from the realm to which the princesses travel at night. He refuses to be paid for keeping their secret, showing his potential as a suitor, not merely a gardener. Oxford, Bodleian Library, Walpole e.411, p. 8.

the German tale the soldier chooses to marry the eldest daughter because he is himself 'not very young', Michael, whom the narration repeatedly describes as a 'boy', gradually wins the affections of the youngest, Princess Lina, and marries her by mutual decision.[106] This focus on Michael's youth seems to acknowledge the child readership of the Coloured Fairy Books and emphasizes his beauty, intelligence, generosity and humility in ways that do not appear in Grimm – portraying Michael instead as a deserving *fin de siècle* hero who models the looks and behaviour that the Langs' young audience should aspire to. Michael's deference to the princesses' royal stature, and his willingness to suffer their taunts in silence, reflect the class divisions of Victorian society. At the same time, his elevation to royalty – and Lina's declaration that she would rather 'marry a gardener' than see Michael in danger – suggest that in that time of empire and industrial growth any British boy might dream of becoming a gentleman through the right combination of high feeling, impeccable behaviour and shrewd action. (Well, almost any boy, as I will discuss below.)

Other stories aimed at children also convey the importance of generosity and caring for others, at times literalizing the idea of 'giving of yourself' through magical fables and fantastical tales. Oscar Wilde's 'The Happy Prince' (figure 6.4), the title story in his 1888 collection of fairy tales for children, is one example. It features a golden, bejewelled statue of a prince, known in life as the Happy Prince, who weeps at the state of the desperate people he can see from his perch over the city. His weeping brings him into conversation with a swallow resting at his feet, which the prince convinces to pluck out his jewels to deliver to the needy on successive nights. The swallow and the prince fall in love through their shared efforts, which eventually include the bird peeling off all the statue's gold leaf to deliver to hungry children and their families. 'Leaf after leaf of the fine gold he brought to the poor, and the children's faces grew rosier, and they laughed and played games in the street. "We have bread now!" they cried.' When the frost and snow arrive, the swallow, who has delayed his migration south to remain with the prince, finally succumbs to the cold. The bird places a kiss on the statue's mouth before falling down 'dead at his feet', and the Happy Prince's leaden heart 'snaps right in two'. The fragments of heart and the bird's body are joined after death on the dust heap, and again in heaven when chosen by an angel as 'the two most precious things in the city'.[107]

6.4 Oscar Wilde's 'The Happy Prince' has retained its popularity since its first publication in 1888. This children's edition, published by Powell Perry, includes bold illustrations by Angela Baynes, whose sister Pauline famously illustrated works for both C.S. Lewis and J.R.R. Tolkien. Oxford, Bodleian Library, Opie AA 523 (pages unnumbered).

" Who are you ? " he said.

" I am the Happy Prince."

" Why are you weeping then ? " asked the Swallow ; " you have quite drenched me."

This book remained in print throughout and following the period of Wilde's 1895 prosecution for acts of so-called 'gross indecency' with other men, and was reprinted and issued as a classic for children through to the 1960s, when the Westminster Parliament began to reform the homophobic laws that had led to Wilde's imprisonment.[108] The continued popularity of and widespread admiration for Wilde's stories despite his social ruin at the time speak to their status as literary works that convey socially important values to children. The love story between the male statue and male bird is inextricable from the tale's larger message about the importance of compassion and selflessness, as well as its damning critique of officials and structures of power that necessitate and increase the suffering of the many. In Wilde's tale, God himself approves the statue and bird's tragic love, which blossoms across traditional boundaries of gender, species and even living/non-living matter, and emerges through acts of generosity towards the poor, the sick, artists, children and other vulnerable people who live on the margins of society. The fact that this story and the rest of the volume not only remained in circulation through the sexual scandal associated with its author, but was reissued with new illustrations in beautiful editions for children, collectors, the Christmas market and more, is a testament to the extent to which *The Happy Prince and Other Tales* was seen as a powerful material and textual gift for generations of readers.

More recent examples of children's books that feature literal giving of oneself include Philip Pullman's *The Scarecrow and His Servant* (2004), about a self-deluded but kind-hearted scarecrow who, with the help of his boy assistant Jack (a Sancho Panza to his Don Quixote), disrupts the corrupt Buffaloni family's stranglehold over the political, legal and economic systems in their fairy-tale land. In a crucial episode of the story the Scarecrow insists that Jack eat pieces of his turnip head to survive their time on a deserted island, and also overcomes his long-standing dislike of birds to protect a nest of eggs. The Scarecrow and Jack each prioritize vulnerable youth (the unhatched chicks) over their own desires – in the Scarecrow's case, his need to scare birds, and in Jack's, profound hunger – and this results in an alliance with birds that leads to the book's happy ending. Unlike in 'The Happy Prince', the Scarecrow's depleted body can be renewed, and Jack soon finds him a sturdy coconut to replace the turnip when it disintegrates.

Similar acts of self-sacrifice and replenishment in children's literature can be found outside the Anglo-American context, as well: one of the most popular children's characters in Japan, for example, is Anpanman, a kindly superhero whose head is made of *anpan*, a soft bun filled with sweet red bean paste. Anpanman spends his time helping others, including breaking off pieces of his own head for the hungry, and his friends bake him new ones as needed. Originally written as a children's book series by Takashi Yanase in the 1970s, Anpanman also appears in television, films, and on virtually every kind of children's merchandise, and has been Japan's top-grossing character since 2002. This emphasis on generosity in Japanese culture has, as in the English examples, numerous historical precedents in Japanese traditional fables. From Continental Europe, Swiss author Marcus Pfister's multi-award-winning 1992 picture book *Der Regenbogenfisch* (*The Rainbow Fish*) features a multicoloured fish who decides to share his beautiful shiny scales with the other fish. After this distribution the Rainbow Fish, like all the other fish, has just one shiny scale, but many friends. This book has been widely translated and adapted, and (likely in response to criticism of the book as promoting socialist or collectivist values) Pfister's website includes a note claiming that it 'has no political message. The story only wants to show us the joy of sharing.'[109] Pfister's emphasis on teaching children that generosity is both a virtue and a pathway to happiness echoes earlier combinations of instruction and delight in children's literature. While young readers may enjoy the bright colours and flashing foil scales of the book for a time, Pfister seems to hope that the moral behind the narrative will remain a gift that keeps giving throughout his young readers' lives.

'Sons of Adam and daughters of Eve': fantasy and cultural inheritance

The growth of children's literature as its own kind of writing, to be developed and gifted to youth for the purposes of teaching and delighting them, is inevitably related to the modern understanding of childhood by which children *themselves* are gifts: precious, innocent responsibilities that must be nurtured by their families and societies. In his 'Ode on Intimations of Immortality from Recollections of Early Childhood' (1804) William Wordsworth famously describes babies arriving at birth 'trailing clouds of glory … / From God, who is our home', highlighting children's divine nature and delivery to mortality as a kind of gift, or perhaps a blessed loan, from heaven.[110] In this, Wordsworth attributes to all children echoes of the heavenly gift that, according to Christian tradition, God gave to humanity through the birth of Jesus.

So it is perhaps unsurprising that one of the most iconic modern fairy stories in the Anglo-American tradition, C.S. Lewis's 1950 children's novel *The Lion, the Witch and the Wardrobe*, unfolds in a magical otherworld where it is 'always winter, and never Christmas', with four English children from our own world as the heroes.[111] The Pevensie siblings save that land, Narnia, from the grip of an authoritarian witch by aligning themselves with the allegorical Christ figure Aslan, who takes the form of a lion and repeats the Christian narrative of self-sacrifice on behalf of erring humans (in this case, one of the children). As in the story of Crucifixion and Resurrection, Aslan is humiliated and put to death at the hands of the witch and her supporters, then returns to life more powerful than before and in this state leads the children and loyal Narnians to defeat her army (figure 6.5). The idea of self-sacrifice as the ultimate gift appears in numerous religious traditions and is discussed in Chapters 2 and 3 of this volume; in its Christian form it recurs in many Western works for children. This is true for texts that explicitly refer to God, like 'The Happy Prince'; allegories like *The Lion, the Witch and the Wardrobe*, in which the Pevensie children are received by Narnians as 'sons of Adam and daughters of Eve'; and ostensibly secular tales like J.K. Rowling's popular *Harry Potter* series, which comes to a close through a sequence that includes Harry's martyrdom, magical resurrection and an ensuing battle.

Fantasy and fairy tales' ability to convey the power of the Christian story in fresh ways was something that drew together C.S. Lewis and his friend, colleague and fellow Inkling J.R.R. Tolkien while they were both teaching at the University of Oxford. In fact, it was by convincing Lewis of this capacity that Tolkien famously helped to convert his friend back to Christianity. These men are best known today for their fiction, and are hailed as fathers of the modern fantasy genre. While Tolkien claimed not to like the kind of obvious allegory that Lewis used in *The Lion, the Witch and the Wardrobe*, he wrote about the power of what he called 'eucatastrophe' in fairy tales: the 'sudden joyous "turn"' in stories, when a happy ending emerges against all odds. In his essay 'On Fairy-Stories' Tolkien calls the Christian story 'the greatest and most complete conceivable eucatastrophe', and argues that

6.5 Pauline Baynes's illustration of the sacrifice of Aslan, from C.S. Lewis's *The Lion, The Witch and the Wardrobe*. The narrative here alludes to the stories of Abraham and Isaac and of the Crucifixion, closely linked in the medieval Christian traditions that Lewis studied and taught at Oxford and Cambridge.

the uplifting, hopeful feelings that come with reading such joyful turns in fiction can offer 'a fleeting glimpse of Joy, Joy beyond the walls of the world, poignant as grief'.[112] Tolkien's 1937 children's novel *The Hobbit* was the first of his works dedicated to the history and mythology of the imaginary fantasy realm known as Middle-earth, which avoided explicit mention of Christianity but included many such moments of triumph snatched from the jaws of defeat.

Middle-earth, which comes from the Old English term *middangeard* (literally meaning 'middle enclosure') is a magical world modelled on premodern Europe and filled with references to the medieval literature that Tolkien and Lewis studied and taught. For instance, *The Hobbit* includes a dangerous dragon who lays waste to the land because he discovers a cup has been stolen from among his treasures; this same scenario plays out in *Beowulf*, the great Old English poem that Tolkien and Lewis made a set text in the Oxford English curriculum that they overhauled, starting in 1930 (figure. 6.6). The magical ring that first appears in *The Hobbit* and motivates the action of Tolkien's *The Lord of the Rings* has been widely seen as modelled on the ring in the medieval Icelandic tale of Sigurd in the *Volsunga Saga* and its Germanic parallels; every version of this tale also involves overcoming a dragon who is guarding an immense hoard. As a result, children's fantasy writings like *The Hobbit* that draw upon medieval tales can convey social values to young readers, but also give them glimpses of a cultural and historical tradition, through the enjoyment of an adventure tale. Indeed, this 'gift' of cultural legacy is one that Tolkien received through his own childhood reading: Andrew Lang's adaptation of the story of Sigurd for the *Red Fairy Book* was reportedly one of Tolkien's favourites as a boy.

The idea that children's literature can be books of mythic knowledge and cultural inheritance that guide young people (who are themselves near-magical gifts to the world, as they grow into adulthood and usher in better futures) appears *inside* children's literature, as well. Child characters in fantasy, especially, often gain essential knowledge from other books of legend and fairy tale. This is a frequent device in works by authors who studied under Tolkien and Lewis's curriculum at Oxford.[113] For example, Susan Cooper, who attended the University between 1953 and 1956, includes a magical book called 'the Book of Gramarye' in her novel *The Dark Is Rising* (1973), the best known of her Arthurian sequence by the same name.

6.6 In J.R.R. Tolkien's *The Hobbit*, Smaug the dragon guards a glistening hoard of treasure, his greed being the antithesis of the hobbit Bilbo Baggins's generosity and self-sacrifice. Oxford, Bodleian Library, MS. Tolkien Drawings 30.

Conversation with Smaug

6.7 A gift that also demonstrates Lyra's special gifts of insight and courage, the alethiometer is an important part of Philip Pullman's *His Dark Materials* trilogy. This is a replica of the instrument described in the books, and was commissioned by Pullman from artist Tony Thomson in 2008.

When the English protagonist Will reads from this ancient volume as part of his training and initiation as a magical 'Old One', text and experience collide: snatches of language from known British works ranging from Old English riddles to twentieth-century poetry transform into embodied knowledge, unlocking the boy's latent abilities as a defender of the 'Light'. In *Fire and Hemlock* (1985), Diana Wynne Jones, who also studied English at Oxford, 1953–56, retells the 'Tam Lin' border ballad in a modern setting. In that novel, the Tam Lin character sends the girl Polly an unofficial curriculum of books of adventure stories, fairy tales, fantasy and children's literature over the years in the hope that they will help her recognize the terms of his magical bondage (they do). In these and other works, books are often gifts of inheritance and power that child readers use to help them on the way to heroic action. Other fantasy by authors from Ursula Le Guin to

J.K. Rowling similarly reinforce the idea that literature, reading and books – especially old ones, or ones that engage with old knowledge – can be magical in and of themselves and are doubly powerful forces for good when wielded by children as part of their learning.

Philip Pullman, who completed his Oxford English degree in 1968, is best known for the fantastical *His Dark Materials* trilogy (1995–2000) and accompanying volumes, which famously rebel against Christianity and the conservative social values that tend to dominate fantasy. So these books may also be expected to undermine the idea of English literary inheritance as a perfect training ground for young heroes. But while the trilogy does set aside the medieval landscapes typical of twentieth-century fantasy, a good part of the action takes place amidst the dreaming spires of Oxford itself, and the narrative builds on Milton's *Paradise Lost*, an important text in the syllabus Pullman studied at Oxford. His protagonist Lyra does not encounter a book of legendary guidance, but is given a magic symbol-reader, called the alethiometer, in the first volume (figure 6.7). In a reversal of the Victorian 'toy' books discussed above, the alethiometer works as a kind of toy or gadget that can function like a book: Lyra learns to 'read' the truth in this 'golden compass' by interpreting the symbols' meanings in combination and in diverse contexts. In an echo of *The Lion, the Witch and the Wardrobe*'s references to Genesis, Lyra emerges as a 'second Eve' who saves the universe; but in this case through the power of 'true stories' about passionate and fully lived lives rather than through adherence to traditional religious myths.

Exclusion and transformation: racial legacies and expanded myths of the gift

As well known and beloved as they both are, neither the idea of children as precious gifts to the world nor the fantasy tradition of child protagonists as natural heroes have historically extended to all children. In fact, at the same time as understandings of childhood as a precious gift from heaven were sweeping Britain and the United States in the eighteenth and nineteenth centuries, Black and Brown children could – and often did – function as an entirely different sort of gift. As literal property in British colonies and the USA, enslaved children were valued at a currency amount and, as Faith Binckes discusses in the previous chapter, were often passed down as a form of inheritance within families, including to other (White) children.[114]

Modern notions of 'the child' have always been implicitly raced White, excluding other children from the category of childhood in ways that continue to have painful effects today.[115] These include disproportionate punishment in school and legal contexts, and widespread assumptions that Black and Brown young people are older and less innocent than their White peers. Evidence of such racial exclusion from childhood appears throughout children's literature itself, including in fantastical tales of other times and worlds. For example, Michael is not the only boy to appear in the Langs' version of 'The Twelve Dancing Princesses': the magical castle where the princesses dance is staffed by 'negro boys' who serve Michael and the other guests. The fates of these unnamed 'black pages' are not discussed when the spell breaks and the princesses leave that land for ever.[116]

Abolitionists would sometimes try to harness the outpouring of everyday sentiment on behalf of White children to create empathy for enslaved Black youth, describing harrowing scenes of babies torn from their mothers and other inhumane circumstances that these children endured. In one campaign, American abolitionists commissioned photographs of light-skinned children from New Orleans who had recently been emancipated, prettily dressed and described in ways that encourage White readers to see them *as* children. In one photo from 1863 (figure 6.8), a light-skinned girl named Rosa and a dark-skinned boy named Isaac share the frame, and their descriptions in an 1864 *Harper's Weekly* article paint both children's personal and academic qualities in glowing terms – as if to dare viewers who find sympathetic parallels between pale Rosa and the children of their own acquaintance to find reason not to extend this sympathy to Isaac and all children, whatever their colour.

Even after emancipation, however, Anglo-American children's and popular literature continued to reproduce racist norms that excluded or demeaned Black, Brown, Asian and Indigenous characters well into the twentieth century. From the minstrel-faced 'golliwog' toys in Enid Blyton's Noddy series to the 'half-troll' black men from Far Harad in Tolkien's *Lord of the Rings*, 'innocent' children's books and fantasy works were often anything but to the readers who found only distorted images of themselves there – if they found characters who looked like them at all.[117] The gifts of enjoyment, passed-down knowledge, and sense of natural cultural inheritance that such books represent for many White children can therefore take on very different meanings in the hands of readers who know

Isaac & Rosa, Slave Children from New Orleans.
PHOTOGRAPHED BY KIMBALL, 477 BROADWAY, N. Y.
Ent'd accord'g to act of Congress in the year 1863, by GEO. H.
HANES, in the Clerk's Office of the U.S for the So. Dist.of N. Y.

themselves to fall outside this constructed racial category. In response, some authors have creatively adapted and reframed the norms of children's literature, including fantasy, to be more representative of the people and histories that are just as crucial to the Anglo-American story. Far from simply dropping characters with these racial and ethnic identities into traditional fantasy contexts, such books create new settings where young protagonists can learn about the historical violence that their forebears experienced, and through this reckoning unlock the unique magical

6.8 This card was produced by abolitionists to inspire sympathy for enslaved children, deliberately placing a light-skinned and dark-skinned child side by side, while an accompanying article praises their personal qualities. *Carte de visite* of emancipated children Isaac and Rosa, New York, 1863 (photographed by Myron H. Kimball). The Gilder Lehrman Institute of American History, GLC05111.02.1051.

capabilities that they too have inherited. These literary and generic developments contribute to an ever-widening horizon of cultural gifts and moments of transformative exchange for young readers to discover and engage in.

Canadian-American author Zetta Elliott's 2017 middle-grade novel *The Ghosts in the Castle* tells the story of a fantasy-loving Black girl named Zaria from New York who is visiting her family, descendants of the Caribbean-born Windrush generation, in London for the summer. There she learns about the painful history of colonialism that hovers behind the opulence of the real-world castles, royal jewels and noble titles that fill her favourite books. On a tour of Windsor Castle she meets the ghosts of Prince Alemayehu of Ethiopia and Sarah Forbes Bonetta Davies, from what is now Nigeria, both of whom were brought as children to England, where Queen Victoria took particular interest in them. While Sarah's ghost (known as Sally in the novel) is able to travel between locations from her remarkable life, Alemayehu, who died at just 18, sorrowfully haunts the castle buildings at Windsor, where he was buried (and remains today, in spite of requests from the Ethiopian government to repatriate his body). Sally tells Zaria and her cousin Winston to help Alemayehu 'hold onto that which binds him to home'.[118] After a visit to the Black Cultural Archives, where the children learn about the thousands of other Black Britons who have lived in the UK over hundreds of years, they make a trip to Brixton Market. There they buy gifts for Alemayehu: an Ethiopian-made *shamma* cloth, frankincense and myrrh-scented oil, and a popular Ethiopian snack called *kolo* (figure 6.9). Armed with these multisensory reminders of the prince's homeland, the children call him with the scent of the oil, then ask him to share memories of his mother and the legend of Makeda, Queen of Sheba, that she used to tell him as a small boy. As he revels in the flavour of berbere and the tale of his ancestor, Alemayehu regains the joyful qualities of his childhood self and finally, with the *shamma* cloth wrapped around his shoulders, walks off hand in

6.9 Artist Charity Russell provided illustrations for Zetta Elliott's *The Ghosts in the Castle* (2017). Here, she shows the book's American and British protagonists Zaria and Winston choosing an Ethiopian *shamma* cloth in a shop near Brixton market in London. They will later give it to the ghost of Prince Alemayehu. *The Ghosts in the Castle* (Rosetta Press), p. 79.

hand with Sally – presumably back to the land from which he was taken so long ago.

Zaria and Winston's adventure teaches them that African legends, objects, and experiences can hold their own potent magic; and that discovering, celebrating, and sharing their places in the Anglo-American world can be part of the larger work of acknowledging and repairing deep colonial harms, whose effects still resonate in contemporary institutions. Indeed, much of the art, manuscripts and other cultural items seized in Ethiopia during the Napier expedition of 1868 – the same military intervention that brought Prince Alemayehu to England – were subsequently acquired or sold on privately in Britain and are now held in libraries and museums in the UK. These include the British Museum, the British Library, the Victoria and Albert Museum and the Bodleian. Telling the difficult stories of such holdings and histories can form part of a process of healing and imagining better futures together. Such futures do not have to leave behind all that has come before; on the contrary, books like *The Ghosts in the Castle* joyfully participate in the children's fantasy genre even as they transform it.

Tracy Deonn's 2020 young adult novel *Legendborn* is an Arthurian retelling that both honours and transforms the cultural gift of legends like those known as the 'Matter of Britain' by exploring what the 'gifts' of blood and cultural inheritance that are so important to medievalist fantasy might look like for a Black character. The novel's heroine is Bree, a 16-year-old Black girl, who stumbles across a secret Arthurian society (the Legendborn) while attending an early college programme at the University of North Carolina at Chapel Hill. This all-White community is made up of the teen- and college-aged descendants of the Knights of the Round Table and their vassal families, who use inherited magic to fight demons known as the Shadowborn. Bree proves mysteriously able to see and resist Legendborn magic, and later joins the society with the support of her budding love interest Nick, who also happens to be the reluctant heir apparent to Arthur. The seemingly righteous organization greets her training with both open and veiled forms of racism, and there is no magical tome that inducts Bree in the ways of the Legendborn. Instead, by engaging antebellum history with the help of other Black women, Bree learns to understand and interpret a different kind of text: the multilayered histories embedded in her own DNA.

As it turns out, Nick is not Arthur's heir, but Bree is, due to the underdiscussed but widespread genetic intermingling of enslaver and enslaved through the systemic rape of Black women in the chattel slavery system. Bree also discovers that she possesses a secret form of magic called rootcraft that passes between generations of Black women, who view the 'colonizer magic' of the Legendborn with revulsion. A hybrid of both, Bree must decide whether or not to accept her unasked-for Arthurian powers and all that they stand for. Rather than a welcome gift, her ability to embody the 'once and future king' is, as Deonn's novel puts it, 'A legacy forced, not given'.[119] In its Arthurian adaptation *Legendborn* not only reframes these iconic medieval legends as belonging as much to the children of Black, Indigenous and other colonized communities as to the descendants of White families who claim to be able to trace their bloodlines back to English nobility. It also brings into fresh view the moral ambivalence about Arthur and his Round Table that appears in many actual medieval Arthurian works.

Other children's and young adult speculative fiction, like Nnedi Okorafor's *Binti Trilogy* (figure 6.10) and Métis author Cherie Dimaline's *The Marrow Thieves*, look outside medieval European source texts to propose legendary foundations for magic that demonstrate some of the ways in which Black, Brown, Asian and Indigenous youth carry equally powerful gifts of legend, belief and ability in their family heritages. Such works echo the adult hopes for children evident in volumes like *Peter Parley's Annual* and *The Christmas Box*: that, by providing young people with reading options created specifically with them in mind, they will not only find enjoyment but also learn about who they are – and who they might be – in the complex world that they are inheriting. Children's access to books is, of course, wildly unequal, and so charities such as Booktrust, the Children's Book Project, Dolly Parton's Imagination Library, Give a Book and others work to put children's literature into the hands and homes of all kids. Such gifts increase home libraries, the size of which has been correlated with greater literacy, numeracy and technological skills in young people even after correcting for socio-economic factors and family educational attainment levels. Further, they continue the tradition of recognizing the individual personhood of children by giving books that bring knowledge and, hopefully, delight to young readers. And, by introducing kids to stories that reflect social values like generosity and courage, these gifts also implicitly invite young people to engage with what their societies hold dear – and ideally encourage them to take part in rethinking and rewriting our evolving cultural narratives.

6.10 Nnedi Okorafor's *Binti* (2015) is the first of a series of science-fiction novellas focusing on Binti, a young Himba woman with extraordinary gifts, who in this book sets out for the intergalactic university Oomza Uni.

HUGO AND NEBULA AWARD-WINNER!

BINTI

Nnedi Okorafor

"There's more vivid imagination in a page of Nnedi Okorafor's work
than in whole volumes of ordinary fantasy epics." — Ursula K. Le Guin

THE JAPANESE HOUSE

MATERIAL CULTURE IN THE MODERN HOME

Inge Daniels
Photography by Susan Andrews

Chapter 7

Two Cups, a Shell and Some Books: Reflections on Anthropology and Gifting

Inge Daniels

Cups, funerals and friendship

On 31 March 2015 my dear friend and mentor Yutaka Kagemori passed away. Two weeks earlier I had found myself in my local post office in London, frantically trying to beat closing time, packing and posting a treasured gift straight to his hospital bed in Osaka. Yutaka-san had only recently fallen ill, but his health was quickly deteriorating, and Noriko-san, his wife, had asked me with some urgency to post another copy of my book *The Japanese House*.[120] Later she recounted how in his final days he had strategically placed my gift on his bedside table to distract medical staff and visitors with stories and photos of his family home.

For more than twenty-five years the Kagemoris have been generous supporters and fierce reviewers of my research in Japan. They were instrumental to the completion of my first book, which explores the complexities of everyday life in Japanese homes, and I had gifted them, like many other participants in my research, a copy. These gifts were treasured and shared much like family photo albums of days past: the book's descriptions and pictures formed a record of domestic family life that had since – through graduations, weddings and funerals – irreversibly changed. Some, such as the Nishiki family, had created a special alcove for the book in their recently refurbished home; others, such as the Takahashis, had circulated photocopied versions to family and friends. Many of the books described in this Bodleian volume were marked out as valuable gifts, often exquisitely made, from their inception. But books, like my academic monograph, also acquire new connotations when they pass as gifts between owners and readers.

Gifts are intricately entangled with the anthropological project. Not only has it been a topic of intense analysis and theorization over the past 100 years, but gift exchange also facilitates our trademark empirical research, often in challenging locations. Gifts can smooth awkward, introductory encounters between anthropologists and local communities;

7.1 The two cups given to Inge Daniels by the Kagemoris as a funerary return-gift, made by Yutaka's sister, and a copy of her book, *The Japanese House*, to which the family contributed so much as participants in the research.

they also aid in maintaining and expanding networks of support over time. However, our anthropological outcomes – books and essays but also films, exhibitions and conferences – have been (and still are?) rarely shared with the people without whom it would have been impossible to build and secure our careers.[121] When I returned my book to them, it gave Yutaka-san and other Japanese families the opportunity to scrutinize my research, but also to shape their own narratives and make their own uses of my book about their lives, including their gift exchanges.

The widespread use of globally connected digital technologies has greatly improved access to anthropological research but a more proactive approach is still needed. Anthropologists linked with museums have long shown that objects, images and texts associated with anthropological knowledge production may have a lasting impact on communities, whose practices and expertise were key to their creation, when they are eventually returned. Thus, monographs may be used, many decades later, to ascertain knowledge hierarchies and create evidence of customary rights in legal disputes.[122] My Ph.D. dissertation, by contrast, gained commercial significance when its main protagonists, Japanese entrepreneurs whose livelihoods depend on tourism, photocopied numerous pages (with images) and hung them in their shopfront windows to sell as souvenirs.[123]

Six months after Yutaka-san died, a package arrived from Japan. Inside were two beautiful ceramic cups. He had instructed his sister, an established potter, to craft fifteen cups to give to his dearest friends. In Japan 'return-gifts' are common at lifecycle events; they are roughly half of the value of the original (money) gifts the recipient had parted with. Through their association with the dead, funerary return-gifts are inauspicious and generally people give perishables or things that easily wear or break. Still, many people, including the Kagemoris, also want to commemorate their deceased loved ones. Yutaka-san's funerary cups straddle both sentiments: they conjure up memories, but they may also break through use.[124]

Yutaka-san was a humble man. He did not want a 'standard' Japanese funeral, a formal affair with the stress on professional achievements. He was a much-loved Geography teacher and a dedicated member of numerous educational bodies, and his memorial service would without a doubt have attracted large crowds. He preferred, instead, to be celebrated with an intimate feast for his wife, daughter and close friends. In the final days of his life, he also selected a few treasured objects, including my book, to take with him on his final journey. I hope that his 'Japanese House' may have eased his passage into the great unknown.

Shells, prestige and (common) wealth

Book gifts are valued well beyond their contents or price in many cultural contexts, but Yutaka's story demonstrates that the personal relationships they embody and mark can also last beyond the grave. The cups, his funerary return-gifts, further illustrate the complexities of gifting in Japan, an industrialized, capitalist society where gifts play a key role in the (re)production of the social, economic and cosmic order.[125] The scale and impact of the Japanese gift economy is far more prominent than gifting in Euro-American contexts. Throughout the year, ritual events that necessitate gifting follow each other in quick succession. Japanese gift exchange is characterized by a creative blurring of gifts and commodities that transcends the dichotomies that are common in Euro-American contexts between personal and spontaneous exchanges, and monetary or instrumental ones. Businesses both supply materials and ingredients and pass on knowledge necessary to perform rituals. They also create new gift occasions in line with social change and shifts in taste – such as White Day on 14 March when men are expected to reciprocate the gift of chocolates they may receive from women on Valentine's Day.[126]

Japanese gift practices also challenge classic anthropological theories about gifting that distinguish between 'primitive' gift economies and 'modern' capitalist societies. Shells, like the *mwali* armband depicted overleaf, play a starring role in these ongoing debates about gifting. These beautiful ornaments are ceremonial gifts that were exchanged between powerful men living on a group of islands in Melanesia. Highly ranked shell valuables became imbued with their owners' fame: these shells in effect told the stories of their accomplishments. When they changed hands, their reputation spread across the archipelago. During the 1920s two anthropological 'Big Men' compared this elaborate system of exchange, called the 'Kula Ring', with trade relations in capitalist economies. Bronisław Malinowski contrasted subsistence communities that have moral economies, grounded in a strong social contract between all community members, with capitalist societies that are driven by self-interest and economic rationality and insist on separating social and economic spheres of life.[127] Marcel Mauss, by contrast, argued that principles of obligation and

7.2 A shell armband (*mwali*), decorated with seeds and beads. This was probably used in the famous Kula exchange of the Massim archipelago, including the Trobriand Islands, of Papua New Guinea. Red shell necklaces (*soulava*) are exchanged in return. This armband is believed to have been acquired by Miss E.E. Gage-Brown, a teacher and missionary, who gave it to the Pitt Rivers Museum. Oxford, Pitt Rivers Museum, 1933.40.18.

social integration are part of the overall system of any economy.[128] In the torrent of books and essays on gifts and commodities that have flowed after the work of Mauss and Malinowski, debates about whether a 'free gift' truly exists, and how self-interested commodity exchange is, still continue.[129]

This book as a whole has explored not only public and celebrated books and gifts, but also everyday or intimate exchanges, like the Herricks sending food to their children in Elizabethan London (Chapter 4). While much discussion of Kula dwelt on exchange between powerful men, and the stories that this created, in the 1980s two female anthropologists directed our attention to a more complex and varied set of exchanges, often involving women. Annette Weiner focused on 'inalienable possessions' – showing that many precious items, such as shell valuables (but also land, bones or minerals) were carefully preserved across generations, and only yielded up to exchange when needed to achieve the highest renown as the shell travelled to far-away places, spreading its owners' fame. Weiner shows that in the many subtle moves that constitute such exchange, women play key roles in generating and then preserving objects that are vital to families' and communities' identities and renown.[130] Nancy Munn's work focused on the way in which, in one particular island called Gawa, armband shells were converted through a series of exchanges for food and labour into material wealth (canoes). Eventually, via exchanges of shells, this material wealth returns to the island in the form of symbolic wealth or fame. Like Weiner, Munn highlights the vital roles that women play in Kula exchange; through making and exchanging of materials, food and hospitality (or witchcraft) they enable the redistribution of wealth in the community.[131]

The myriad questions raised by a Kula armlet like this one can then change our attitude to public ceremonies of exchange, and private preservation of books and treasures in families and communities. It can help expand our focus to include not only the beautiful and expensive gift-books presented to royalty or dedicated to the gods, but to the innumerable acts of exchange and shared knowledge, at all levels, that the books and objects in this study hint at.

Kula exchange is competitive and creates status hierarchies, but it does not destroy the common wealth. Mauss identified a 'spirit of the gift' in the non-European societies that he studied: a force that moved people to pass on the benefit of a gift they had received, so that its value or surplus could circulate and return in a cycle of acts and exchanges.[132] The idea that generosity will return, sometimes in unexpected ways, is also found in Euro-American societies; it is embedded in many stories, including in some of the fictions for younger readers discussed in Chapter 6. A state-backed system of taxes and benefits (the 'welfare state') can take on this role too. How far it can or should, however, is a matter of negotiation and controversy.[133]

Books, charity and palaces for the people

In the twenty-first century governments have often seemed impotent or passive in the face of inequality, exploitation and the unsustainable depletion of natural resources. The Covid pandemic, however, has shifted our understanding of what (some) governments are capable of in an emergency, and also of the capacity that ordinary citizens have for acts of generosity and solidarity.[134] A local example is the Oxford Hub, a charity that grew out of student charitable groups, and that draws on volunteers to run a range of programmes aiming to make Oxford a more equal city. During the pandemic it launched 'Oxford Together', a campaign that mobilized more than 5,000 volunteers to deliver emergency goods such as food and medicines. It also supported local residents who were shielding, such as 81-year-old Carl. A series of notes stuck to his door put out a call for books to keep him from boredom, and many people stepped in to offer some. What makes the book such a potent charitable gift is not only its function as container of a huge variety of stories and knowledge that each reader may or may not appreciate according to their own interests and experiences, but also its materiality as a portable object that does not decay easily and is relatively cheap.

7.3 In the first wave of the Covid-19 pandemic in 2020, Oxford Hub asked for donations of books for Carl, an Oxford resident who was isolating and bored. The immediate response was just one of countless acts of generosity amidst the Covid crisis. Photos © Sara Fernandez, illustration by Bluetiful Designs for Oxford Hub.

Keep Oxfam in action— spreading knowledge in the hungry half of the world

Another organization with roots in Oxford that is perhaps better known for offering assistance in times of crisis is Oxfam. This charity was founded in the 1940s by a mixed group of Quakers, academics and social activists. Initially the focus was on addressing famine and destitution in Europe, but the organization then began to offer emergency relief during global crises. The 'Oxford Fountain' poster notes that by 1959 donations supported refugees across thirty-five countries. Charity shops became key to Oxfam's success: currently the organization operates more than 1,200 shops worldwide, selling fair-trade items and donated goods. Clothing remains a popular gift (the 'Oxford Fountain' poster mentions 'about 700 tons' of clothing 'for distribution overseas'), but books and knowledge were also framed as 'perfect' charitable gifts. A striking example is a poster from the 1960s showing a Black child writing in a notebook while reading books and the text 'Keep Oxfam in action – spreading knowledge in the hungry half of the world.'

Today Oxfam is part of a global aid industry that depends on people in the global North donating goods and money to help the poor in the global South. The impulse to give freely to impoverished others, linked with ideals of humanitarianism and civil society, is rooted in the Euro-American dichotomous thinking about exchange discussed earlier. Gifts tend to be conceptualized as tokens of love and affection that reference unique, personal relationships as opposed to anonymous commodity exchanges linked with price. The economic anthropologist James Carrier argues that this 'ideology of the free gift' draws on the assumption that people are individual, rational agents free from obligation, and that the economic sphere is separate

7.4 Oxfam (originally Oxford Committee for Famine Relief) was founded in Oxford in 1942. From its early years raising money to relieve suffering in war-torn Europe, Oxfam then became a major global charity, opening the UK's first charity shop in 1948. Oxford, Bodleian Library, MS. Oxfam COM/1/8/2/2 ('Spreading knowledge', 1964; above); MS. Oxfam COM/1/8/197 ('The Oxford Fountain', c.1959; opposite).

ALSO 70 OTHER ORGANIZATIONS
HELPING REFUGEES
ALL OVER
THE WORLD

Refugee Service Committee Greece
Spanish Refugee Aid
Calcutta Christian Fellowship
Maryknoll Sisters
Ockenden Venture
Baptist Missionary Society
Edinburgh Med: Missionary Society
Shatin Babies' Homes
Y.M.C.A. & Y.W.C.A.
Lutheran World Federation
Mrs Donnithorne, Hong Kong
Near East Christian Council

U.N High Commissioner for Refugees
Church Missionary Society
National Catholic Welfare Conference
Tunisian Red Crescent
Friends Service Council
Inter Church Aid
League of Red Cross Societies
Salvation Army
Korean Mission
Korean Church World Service
Bishop Mason, Sudan
National Christian Council of India
Save the Children Fund

OXFORD COMMITTEE for FAMINE RELIEF

GIFTS FROM THE OXFORD COMMITTEE'S
200,000 SUPPORTERS

The OXFORD FOUNTAIN

Some of the 35 countries where Refugees and other
destitute people have been helped :—
Austria, Brazil, Chile, Formosa, France, Germany, Greece, Haiti, Hong Kong
India, Indonesia, Iran, Italy, Jugoslavia, Jordan, Korea, Morocco, Pakistan,
Portugal, Sudan, Tunisia, Vietnam, etc.

CASH GRANTS & **SUPPLIES** for year ended 30 September 1959 · · · · · £182,252
VALUE of **CLOTHING** (about 700 Tons) for distribution overseas for year ended 30 Sept 1959 £248,746
COST of **BALING**, packing, transport & freight   "   "   "   £33,953

NATURE of PROJECTS ASSISTED

Mobile Canteen ·· Vocational Training Centres ·· Hospitals & Clinics ·· Orphanages ·· Loans to set up Refugees
Mobile Dental Centre ·· Old People's Homes ·· Relief of Flood & Earthquake Victims ·· Feeding Schemes ·· Rooftop Schools
Student Work Projects ·· Settlement of handicapped out-of-camp Refugees ·· Building of Cottages ·· Clothing distribution
Provision articulated limbs for Korean amputees ·· Rehabilitation & resettlement ·· Clothing, & Blankets ·· Emigration Passage money.

from other spheres of life.[135] However, free gifts also have unexpected economic, political and ecological consequences. Charitable gifts that travel through long chains of transactions and middlemen may be transformed into interested transactions; they may, for example, end up being redistributed through local relationships of patronage and indebtedness.[136] Emergency relief saves lives, but long-term flooding of local markets with 'humanitarian' goods is often detrimental to local industries.[137] Schemes that encourage local entrepreneurship such as 'bottom of the pyramid' approaches are often lauded as the solution. However, in practice, responsibility for poverty reduction is deflected onto the poor themselves, and new forms of inequality arise between those who are aspirational and active, and the so-called undeserving, unproductive poor.[138]

As governments in the global North implement austerity policies and cut aid budgets, global businesses are increasingly funding, designing and delivering products and services that aim to improve the well-being of disenfranchised people across the globe. Charitable giving by the wealthy has of course a long history in Europe and North America, whether construed as pious acts (for example, bequests to churches) or secular activities. One example is the livery companies in the City of London (based on influential trade groups including the Mercers, Merchant Taylors and Goldsmiths, and now numbering over one hundred) that from their medieval origins have supported almshouses, hospitals, schools and colleges, and still give substantial charitable grants.[139] This legacy has more recently developed into what is called 'philanthro-capitalism' with 'social investing' focusing on providing access to knowledge and education for all. One such example is the organization ARK, which operates a network of thirty-nine schools in the UK, but also works abroad in countries such as India, Indonesia and Ethiopia.[140] Many commercial organizations are making significant contributions to mitigate problems of inequality and/ or environmental damage. However, conflating business techniques with gifting is also criticized for trading in the risk of the poor.[141] Have crises and natural disasters become tax-free investment opportunities that enrich shareholders? Can profit really be squared with elevating poverty? Is this not giving, while taking?

The American sociologist Eric Klinenberg asks similar questions as he bemoans the steady decline of communal spaces, funded and administered by the state (such as parks or libraries) in the USA but also other countries with neo-liberal regimes such as the UK. He calls these spaces, which enable social connections and play a crucial role in individual and collective well-being, 'Palaces for the People'.[142] He argues that the commercial world can play a role in maintaining existing social infrastructures as well as creating new ones, but only if they model themselves on the great nineteenth-century philanthropists who gave to charity without seeing it as a profit-making venture.

He singles out Andrew Carnegie, the Scottish-American industrialist whose many philanthropic achievements included building public libraries. But, closer to home, the Bodleian Library owes much of its position as one of the richest archives in the world to innovators and donors, including Thomas Bodley and other benefactors over the centuries. While the Bodleian is a university library focused on research and teaching, it is making efforts to open its collections to the public too. Such moves can ensure that university libraries, like other kinds of library, become democratic spaces where people of all backgrounds and interests may access the gift of knowledge, and the education imbued in books. As such they are 'the bedrocks of civil society … places where the public, private and philanthropic sectors can work together to reach for something higher than the bottom line'.[143]

Books, then, may be gifts that contain powerful messages about value, solidarity and friendship, resonating across oceans and even beyond the grave. But reflecting on gifts we also need to address questions of hierarchy, ethics and (in)equality. Books and gifts help us to understand the complex networks of obligation and indebtedness in which we all operate, while relishing the spontaneous pleasures of both giving and receiving.

1. S.F. Said, 'The Best Gifts you can Give', in Jenni Orchard (ed.), *The Gifts of Reading: Essays on the Joys of Reading, Giving and Receiving Books*, Weidenfeld & Nicolson, London, 2021, pp. 237–48, at p. 240.

2. Yunxiang Yan, 'Gifts', in Felix Stein (ed.), *The Cambridge Encyclopedia of Anthropology*, http://doi.org/10.29164/20gifts (accessed 4 April 2022); Marcel Mauss, *The Gift: Expanded Edition*, ed. and trans. Jane I. Guyer, Hau Books, Chicago IL, 2016 (first published 1925), p. 61.

3. Mauss, *The Gift*, pp. 69–73. These dynamics are explored in Lewis Hyde's influential *The Gift: How the Creative Spirit Transforms the World*, new edn, Canongate Books, Edinburgh, 2012.

4. See Karen Sykes, *Arguing with Anthropology: An Introduction to Critical Theories of the Gift*, Routledge, London, 2005, pp. 3–4 (quoting p. 3).

5. See Robyn Marsack, *The Tale of 10 Mysterious Sculptures Gifted to the City of Words and Ideas*, Polygon, Edinburgh, 2012, pp. 10–12.

6. Edwin Morgan, *Collected Poems*, Carcanet, Manchester, 1990, p. 519.

7. *Aeneid* 2.40–56, trans. H. Rushton Fairclough, *Virgil: Eclogues. Georgics. Aeneid, Books 1–6*, rev. G.P. Goold, Loeb Classical Library 63, Harvard University Press, Cambridge MA, 1916. For a recent, lively translation, see *The Aeneid. Vergil*, trans. Sarah Ruden, rev. edn, Yale University Press, New Haven CT, 2021.

8. For the priest's grisly fate, see *Aeneid* 2.200–44. For variations of the myth, including Athena's role in devising the horse, see B.A. Sparkes, 'The Trojan Horse in Classical Art', *Greece and Rome*, vol. 18, no. 1, 1971, pp. 54–70; Lauren Murphy, 'Horses, Ships and Earthquakes: The Trojan Horse in Myth and Art', *Iris: Journal of the Classical Association of Victoria* 30, 2017, pp. 18–36.

9. The classic discussion remains Marcel Mauss, *The Gift: Expanded Edition*, ed. and trans. Jane I. Guyer, Hau Books, Chicago IL, 2016 (first published 1925). A useful, open-access overview of subsequent debates and critiques is included in Yunxiang Yan, 'Gifts', in Felix Stein (ed.), *The Cambridge Encyclopedia of Anthropology*: http://doi.org/10.29164/20gifts (accessed 7 May 2022).

10. See Christoph Auffarth, 'Gift and Sacrifice', in Michael Stausberg and Steven Engler (eds), *The Oxford Handbook of the Study of Religion*, Oxford University Press, Oxford, 2017, pp. 541–58. See also more broadly Michael L. Satlow (ed.), *The Gift in Antiquity*, Wiley-Blackwell, Chichester, 2013.

11. Francesca Stavrakopoulou, *God: An Anatomy*, Picador, London, 2021, pp. 211–14.

12. The object is now housed in the Iraq Museum, Baghdad (IM 19606). For its self-referential, performative nature, see Zainab Bahrani, 'Performativity and the Image: Narrative, Representation, and the Uruk Vase', in Erica Ehrenberg (ed.), *Leaving No Stones Unturned: Essays on the Ancient Near East and Egypt in Honor of Donald P. Hansen*, Eisenbrauns, Winona Lake IN, 2002, pp. 15–22.

13. See Christopher Woods, 'The Earliest Mesopotamian Writing', in Christopher Woods (ed.), *Visible Language: Inventions of Writing in the Ancient Middle East and Beyond*, Oriental Institute Museum Publications 32, Oriental Institute of the University of Chicago, Chicago IL, 2010, pp. 33–50; Robert K. Englund, 'Accounting in Proto-Cuneiform', in Karen Radner and Eleanor Robson (eds), *The Oxford Handbook of Cuneiform Culture*, Oxford University Press, Oxford, 2011, pp. 32–50.

14. ETCSL 1.3.1: The Electronic Text Corpus of Sumerian Literature, ed. J.A. Black et al., University of Oxford, 1998–2006, https://etcsl.orinst.ox.ac.uk. For an introductory discussion of the text, and brief explanatory notes, see Samuel Noah Kramer and John Maier, *Myths of Enki, The*

Notes

Crafty God, Oxford University Press, Oxford, 1989; repr. Wipf and Stock, Eugene OR, 2020, pp. 57–68.

15. E.g. ETCSL 1.3.1, section D, lines 6–13.

16. Jean-Jacques Glassner, 'Inanna et les ME', in Maria de Jong Ellis (ed.), *Nippur at the Centennial: Papers Read at the 35e Recontre Assyriologique Internationale*, University of Philadelphia Museum, Philadelphia PA, 1992, pp. 55–86.

17. For recent, accessible translations of these works, see Homer, *The Odyssey*, trans. Emily Wilson, Norton, New York and London, 2018; and Homer, *The Iliad: A New Translation*, trans. Caroline Alexander, Ecco Press, New York, 2015.

18. ETCSL 1.08.01.05. For further discussion about this text and these gifts, see Jon Taylor, 'Two Critical Passages in *Gilgameš and Huwawa*', in Heather D. Baker, Eleanor Robson and Gábor Zólyomi (eds), *Your Praise Is Sweet: A Memorial Volume for Jeremy Black from Students, Colleagues and Friends*, British Institute for the Study of Iraq, London, 2010, pp. 351–60.

19. W.G. Lambert, 'A Catalogue of Texts and Authors', *Journal of Cuneiform Studies*, vol. 16, no. 3, 1962, pp. 59–77.

20. Ashm. 1922.0009, trans. Douglas Frayne, *Ur III Period (2112–2004 BC)*, The Royal Inscriptions of Mesopotamia, Early Periods, volume 3/2, University of Toronto Press, Toronto, 1997, pp. 124–5.

21. Christina Tsouparopoulou, 'Deconstructing Textuality, Reconstructing Materiality', in Thomas E. Balke and Christina Tsouparopoulou (eds), *Materiality of Writing in Early Mesopotamia*, De Gruyter, Berlin, 2016, pp. 257–75 (esp. pp. 268–71).

22. See Karel van der Toorn, *Scribal Culture and the Making of the Hebrew Bible*, Harvard University Press, Cambridge MA, 2007; Michael L. Satlow, *How the Bible Became Holy*, Yale University Press, New Haven CT, 2014.

23. On these motifs in medieval Jewish illuminated manuscripts, and the possibility that these bird-like faces might be better understood as griffin heads, see Marc Michael Epstein, 'Focus: Exploring the Mystery of the Birds' Head Haggadah', in Marc Michael Epstein (ed.), *Skies of Parchment, Seas of Ink: Jewish Illuminated Manuscripts*, Princeton University Press, Princeton NJ, 2015, pp. 97–104.

24. On the difficulties of interpreting this sacrificial scene, see further Katrin Kogman-Appel, 'The Temple of Jerusalem and the Hebrew Millennium in a Thirteenth-Century Jewish Prayer Book', in Annette Hoffmann and Gerhard Wolf (eds), *Jerusalem as Narrative Space/Erzählraum Jerusalem*, Brill, Leiden, 2021, pp. 187–221.

25. Yehuda B. Cohen, *Tangled up in Text: Tefillin and the Ancient World*, Brown University Press, Providence RI, 2008.

26. Francesca Stavrakopoulou, 'Materialism, Materiality, and Biblical Cults of Writing', in Katharine J. Dell and Paul M. Joyce (eds), *Biblical Interpretation and Method: Essays in Honour of John Barton*, Oxford University Press, Oxford, 2013, pp. 223–42.

27. Stanley Frye, *The Sutra of the Wise and the Foolish (Mdo Mdzangs Blun), Or, Ocean of Narratives (Üliger-ün Dalai)*, 3rd edn, Library of Tibetan Works & Archives, Dharamsala, India, 2006, pp. 1, 9–10. Editorial note: Udpala emended to Utpala.

28. The standard edition of the Tibetan version is still Isaak Jakob Schmidt, *'Dzaṅs Blun, oder, Der Weise und der Thor*, Gräff, St Petersburg, 1843. On the composition of this work, see Ulrike Roesler, 'Materialien zur Redaktionsgeschichte des *mDzangs Blun*: Die Selbstaufopferung des Prinzen Sujāta', in Konrad Klaus and Jens-Uwe Hartmann (eds), *Indica et Tibetica: Michael Hahn Felicitation Volume*, Vienna University, Vienna, 2007, pp. 405–14.

29. On the difference between these two genres, see Martin Straube, 'Narratives: South Asia', in *Brill's Encyclopedia of Buddhism, Volume 1: Literature and Languages*, Brill, Leiden, 2015, pp. 489–506, at pp. 489–92.

30. Ibid., p. 489.

31. Ronald Steiner, 'Āryaśūra', in *Brill's Encyclopedia of Buddhism, Volume 2: Lives*, Brill, Leiden, 2019, pp. 70–72, at p. 70.

32. Andrew Skilton, *How the Nāgas Were Pleased*, Clay Sanskrit Library 39, New York University Press and JJC Foundation, New York, 2009, p. 3.

33. Camillo Alessio Formigatti, *A Sanskrit Treasury: A Compendium of Literature from the Clay Sanskrit Library*, Bodleian Library Publishing, Oxford, 2019, p. 156.

34. Sanskrit *yad atra puṇyaṃ tad bhavatv ācāryopādhyāyamātāpitṛ pūrvaṅgamaṃ kṛtvā sakalasattvarāśer / °parirāśer anuttarajñānaphalaṃ prāptam iti*.

35. See Nicholas Perkins, 'Introduction: The Materiality of Medieval Romance and *The Erle of Tolous*', in Nicholas Perkins (ed.), *Medieval Romance and Material Culture*, Brewer, Cambridge, 2015, pp. 1–22, and further references there.

36. *The Erle of Tolous*, in *Codex Ashmole 61: A Compilation of Popular Middle English Verse*, ed. George Shuffleton, Medieval Institute Publications, Kalamazoo MI, 2008, lines 399–402; 405. This edition is based on a different manuscript (also in the Bodleian), but the text here is similar. This Kalamazoo series is freely available online, and includes a wealth of medieval English texts in an approachable form.

37. Marcel Mauss, *The Gift: Expanded Edition*, ed. Jane I. Guyer, Hau Books, Chicago IL, 2016, p. 61.

38. For example in Marilyn Strathern's *The Gender of the Gift: Problems with Women and Problems with Society in Melanesia*, University of California Press, Berkeley CA, 1988; and see Sarah Kay, *The 'Chansons de Geste' in the Age of Romance: Political Fictions*, Oxford University Press, Oxford, 1995.

39. For the interaction between spoken and written forms, see M.T. Clanchy, *From Memory to Written Record: England 1066–1307*, 3rd edn, Wiley-Blackwell, Oxford, 2013.

40. Lines 46–8, in *The Cambridge Old English Reader*, ed. Richard Marsden, 2nd edn, Cambridge University Press, Cambridge, 2015.

41. *Genesis B* is included in *Old Testament Narratives*, ed. and trans. Daniel Anlezark, Harvard University Press, Cambridge MA, 2011.

42. Thomas, *Le Roman de Horn*, ed. Mildred K. Pope, 2 vols, rev. T.B.W. Reid, Blackwell, Oxford, 1955; 1964, line 1182. This rich poem is translated in *The Birth of Romance: An Anthology*, trans. Judith Weiss, Dent Everyman, London, 1992. A Middle English version, *King Horn*, is edited in *Four Romances of England: 'Horn', 'Havelok the Dane', 'Bevis of Hampton', 'Athelston'*, ed. Graham Drake et al., Medieval Institute Publications, Kalamazoo MI, 1997.

43. *The Qur'an*, trans. M.A. Abdel Haleem, Oxford University Press, Oxford, 2008, 2.261, and see this whole passage.

44. The passage on this leaf is 27.27–42. For the spiritual gifts described in mystical verse, see *Islamic Mystical Poetry: Sufi Verse from the Early Mystics to Rumi*, trans. Mahmood Jamal, Penguin, London, 2009.

45. Tipu's life and historiography are much debated. A Muslim, his gifts to Hindu temples are discussed in Mohibul Hassan, *History of Tipu Sultan*, Bibliophile, Calcutta, 1951, pp. 360–61. On his library, see Ursula Sims-Williams, 'Collections within Collections: An Analysis of Tipu Sultan's Library', *Iran*, vol. 59, no. 2, 2021, pp. 287–307.

46. See Theo Martin van Lindt and Robin Meyer, *Armenia: Masterpieces from an Enduring Culture*, Bodleian Library Publishing, Oxford, 2015.

47. Annette B. Weiner, *Inalienable Possessions: The Paradox of Keeping-while-Giving*, University of California Press, Berkeley CA, 1992.

48. See Frederica C.E. Law-Turner, *The Ormesby Psalter: Patrons & Artists in Medieval East Anglia*, Bodleian Library Publishing, Oxford, 2017.

49. Thomas Hoccleve, *The Regiment of Princes*, ed. Charles C. Blyth, Medieval Institute Publications, Kalamazoo MI, 1999, lines 2031–2; see Nicholas Perkins, *Hoccleve's 'Regiment of Princes': Counsel and Constraint*, Brewer, Cambridge, 2001.

50. William Langland, *Piers Plowman: A New Annotated Edition of the C-Text*, ed. Derek Pearsall, 2nd edn, Liverpool University Press, Liverpool, 2008, 3.163, 165. See James Simpson, *An Introduction to 'Piers Plowman'*, 2nd edn, Exeter University Press, Exeter, 2007, for Langland's lively and subtle allegory.

51. Geoffrey Chaucer, *The Canterbury Tales*, ed. Jill Mann, Penguin, Harmondsworth, 2005, 3.1758–60. Harvard University's Chaucer site, www.chaucer.fas.harvard.edu (accessed 20 February 2022), and *The Canterbury Tales: A Selection*, trans. Colin Wilcockson, Penguin, London, 2008, both include text and translation.

52. *John Nichols's The Progresses and Public Processions of Queen Elizabeth I*, ed. Elizabeth Goldring et al., 5 vols, Oxford University Press, Oxford, 2014, vol. I, pp. 127, 129.

53. *The Holie Bible conteynyng the olde Testament and the newe*, Richard Jugge, London, 1568, frontispiece.

54. Gerard Kilroy, 'The Queen's Visit to Oxford in 1566: A Fresh Look at Neglected Manuscript Sources', *Recusant History*, vol. 31, no. 3, 2013, pp. 331–73; Felicity Heal, 'Giving and Receiving on Royal Progress', in Jayne Elizabeth Archer et al. (eds), *The Progresses, Pageants and Entertainments of Queen Elizabeth I*, Oxford University Press, Oxford, 2007, pp. 46–64.

55. Jane A. Lawson (ed.), *The Elizabethan New Year's Gift Exchanges 1559–1603*, British Academy, London, 2013, p. 367.

56. *Edmund Spenser: The Shorter Poems*, ed. William A. Oram et al., Yale University Press, New Haven CT, 1989, pp. 81–2.

57. Desiderius Erasmus, *Collected Works, Volume 39: Colloquies*, trans. C.R. Thompson, University of Toronto Press, Toronto, 1997, pp. 132–65, 176–86. See J.B. Trapp, *Erasmus, Colet and More: The Early Tudor Humanists and Their Books*, British Library, London, 1991.

58. Felicity Heal, *The Power of Gifts: Gift-Exchange in Early Modern England*, Oxford University Press, Oxford, 2014, pp. 13–14.

59. Richard Brathwaite, *The English Gentleman*, John Haviland, London, 1630, p. 270; *The Woorke of the Excellent Philosopher Luicus Annaeus Seneca Concerning Benefyting*, trans. Arthur Golding, John Kingston for John Day, London, 1578; *The Workes of Lucius Annaeus Seneca, both Morall and Naturall*, trans. Thomas Lodge, William Stansby, London, 1614.

60. *The Woorke of the Excellent Philosopher Luicus Annaeus Seneca Concerning Benefyting*, trans. Golding, fol. 6.

61. Francis Peck (ed.), *Desiderata Curiosa*, 2 vols, privately printed, London, 1779, vol. I, p. 49; 'The Instructions of Henry Percy, Ninth Earl of Northumberland, to his Son Algernon Percy', ed. J.H. Markland, *Archaeologia* 1838, p. 342.

62. Desiderius Erasmus, *Collected Works, Volume 3: Correspondence*, trans. R.A.B. Mynors and D.F.S. Thomson, University of Toronto Press, Toronto, 1974, pp. 43–4. On church courts and gifts, see Diana O'Hara, *Courtship and Constraint: Rethinking the Making of Marriage in Tudor England*, Manchester University Press, Manchester, 1988. On informal gift networks, see Ilana Ben-Amos, *The Culture of Giving: Informal Support and Gift-Exchange in Early Modern England*, Cambridge University Press, Cambridge, 2008.

63. William Perkins, *Workes*, John Legat, Cambridge, 1603, p. 472. On food and hospitality, see Felicity Heal, *Hospitality in Early Modern England,* Oxford University Press, Oxford, 1990.

64. Edmund Spenser, *The Faerie Queene*, ed. A.C. Hamilton, rev. Hiroshi Yamashita and Toshiyuki Suzuki, Taylor & Francis, Abingdon, 2013, p. 731.

65. Katie McKeogh, 'Sir Thomas Tresham (1543–1605) and Early Modern Catholic Culture and Identity 1580–1610', D.Phil. thesis, University of Oxford, 2017, pp. 234–7; Jason Scott-Warren, *Shakespeare's First Reader: The Paper Trails of Richard Stonley*, University of Pennsylvania Press, Philadelphia PA, 2019, pp. 121–9.

66. *The Works of Francis Bacon*, ed. James Spedding et al., vol. 10, Cambridge University Press, Cambridge, 1868, p. 253.

67. *The Works of Francis Bacon*, ed. James Spedding et al., vol. 6, Cambridge University Press, Cambridge, 1858, pp. 523–4, 539.

68. Ibid., pp. 507, 400. On Bacon and bribes, see John T. Noonan, *Bribes*, Macmillan, New York, 1984, pp. 350–63.

69. The *Works of Francis Bacon*, vol. 6, pp. 401, 494–5, 408.

70. Linda Levy Peck, *Court Patronage and Corruption in Early Stuart England*, Routledge, London, 1990, especially pp. 107–9; Mark Knights, *Trust and Distrust: Corruption in Office in Britain and its Empire 1600–1850*, Oxford University Press, Oxford, 2021.

71. Francis Bamford (ed.), *A Royalist's Notebook: The Commonplace Book of Sir John Oglander of Nunwell*, Constable, London, 1936, p. 5.

72. Thomas Hobbes, *Leviathan*, Andrew Crooke, London, 1651, pt 1, chs 11, 15; Adam Smith, *The Theory of Moral Sentiments*, ed. D.D. Raphael and A.L. Macfie, Oxford University Press, Oxford, 1976, pp. 50–54. See also Harry Liebersohn, *The Return of the Gift: European History of a Global Idea*, Cambridge University Press, Cambridge, 2012.

73. Avner Offer, 'Between the Gift and the Market: The Economy of Regard', *Economic History Review*, vol. 50, no. 3, 1997, pp. 451–2.

74. Louisa May Alcott, *Little Women; or Meg, Jo, Beth and Amy*, Little, Brown, Boston MA, 1915 (first published 1868–9), pp. 1, 15.

75. Ibid., p. 44.

76. Marcel Mauss, *The Gift: Expanded Edition*, trans. Jane I. Guyer, Hau Books, Chicago IL, 2016.

77. Patrick Scott, 'Gift-Wrapping the Hungry Forties: Format vs. Text in Dickens's Christmas Books', *Victorians Institute Journal* 39, 2011, Digital Annex (accessed 20 May 2022).

78. Lorraine Janzen Kooistra, *Poetry, Pictures, and Popular Publishing: The Illustrated Gift Book and Victorian Visual Culture, 1855–1875*, Ohio University Press, Athens OH, 2011, p. 13.

79. Charles Dickens, *A Christmas Carol & Other Christmas Books*, ed. Robert Douglas-Fairhurst, Oxford University Press, Oxford, 2020, p. 41.

80. Lucy Shaw, 'Wartime Fairy Tales', V&A blog, 18 December 2019, www.vam.ac.uk/blog/museum-life/wartime-fairy-tales (accessed 14 April 2022).

81. Arthur Conan Doyle, *A Study in Scarlet*, ed. Owen Dudley Edwards, Oxford University Press, Oxford, 2008, pp. 19, 21.

82. Ibid., p. 40.

83. Vita Sackville-West, 'Introduction', in *The Annual, Being a Selection from the Forget-Me-Nots, Keepsakes, and other Annuals of the Nineteenth Century*, ed. Dorothy Wellesley, Cobden-Sanderson, London, 1930, p. iv.

84. For example, Katherine D. Harris, *Forget Me Not: The Rise of the British Literary Annual, 1823–1835*, Ohio University Press, Athens OH, 2015; Elaine Arvan-Andrews, 'The "Lure of the Fabulous": Gift-Book Beauties and Charlotte Brontë's Early Heroines', *Women's Writing*, vol. 16, no. 2, 2009, pp. 263–82; Jill Rappoport, *Giving Women: Alliance and Exchange in Victorian Culture*, Oxford University Press, Oxford, 2011; Christine Alexander and Jane Sellars, *The Art of the Brontës*, Cambridge University Press, Cambridge, 1995.

85. Rappoport, *Giving Women*.

86. Charlotte Brontë to George Smith, 17 August 1848, in *The Letters of Charlotte Brontë, with a Selection of Letters by Family and Friends, Volume 2: 1848–1851*, ed. Margaret Smith, Clarendon Press, Oxford, 2000, p. 101.

87. Elizabeth Gaskell to Anna Jameson, 15 November [?1854], in *The Letters of Mrs Gaskell*, ed. J.A.V. Chapple and Arthur Pollard, Manchester University Press, Manchester, 1997, p. 322.

88. Christina Rossetti, *Selected Poems*, ed. Dinah Roe, Penguin Books, London, 2008.

89. Stephanie E. Jones-Rogers, *They Were Her Property: White Women as Slave-Owners in the American South*, Yale University Press, New Haven CT, 2019.

90. William and Ellen Craft, *Running a Thousand Miles for Freedom: Or, the Escape of William and Ellen Craft from Slavery*, William Tweedie, London, 1860, p. 2.

91. See Vincent Carretta, *Equiano, the African: Biography of a Self-Made Man*. University of Georgia Press, Athens GA and London, 2005.

92. Olaudah Equiano, *The Interesting Narrative of the Life of Olaudah Equiano, or Gustavus Vassa, the African: Written by Himself*, printed for and sold by the author, London, 1789, p. 9.

93. Ibid., p. 94.

94. Ibid., p. 134.

95. Thomas Wilson, *The Knowledge and Practice of Christianity Made Easy to the Meanest Capacities: Or, an Essay Towards an Instruction for the Indians*, J. Osborn, London, 1743, p. xi.

96. See Megan Fritz and Frank Fee, 'To Give the Gift of Freedom: Gift Books and the War on Slavery', *American Periodicals*, vol. 23, no. 1, 2013, pp. 60–82.

97. See Ralph Thompson, 'The Liberty Bell and Other Anti-Slavery Gift-Books', New England Quarterly, vol. 7, no. 1, 1934, pp. 154–68.

98. Denae Dyck, 'From Denunciation to Dialogue: Redefining Prophetic Authority in Elizabeth Barrett Browning's "A Curse for a Nation"', Victorian Review, vol. 46, no. 1, 2020, pp. 67–82, at p. 71.

99. Harold Raymond, quoted in 'Our History', National Book Tokens website, www.nationalbooktokens.com/our-values (accessed 20 May 2022).

100. See Encyclopedia of Ephemera, ed. Maurice Rickards, Taylor & Francis, London, 2018; Ann Marika Steiner, 'Book Tokens', in The Oxford Companion to the Book, ed. Michael Suarez and H.R. Woudhuysen, Oxford University Press, Oxford, 2010.

101. See Penny Day, Bonhams Catalogue entry, Modern British and Irish Art, 14 November 2018, www.bonhams.com/auctions/24594/lot/6 (accessed 15 May 2022).

102. Robert MacFarlane, 'The Gifts of Reading', Penguin Books, London, 2017, reprinted in The Gifts of Reading: Essays on the Joys of Reading, Giving and Receiving Books, ed. Jennie Orchard, Weidenfeld & Nicolson, London, 2021, pp. 3–18, at p. 12.

103. Marshall's Christmas Box: A Juvenile Annual, W. Marshall, London, 1832, fol. A2r. See also Peter Hunt, 'Instruction and Delight', in Children's Literature: Approaches and Territories, ed. Janet Maybin and Nicola J. Watson, Palgrave Macmillan/Open University, Basingstoke, 2009, pp. 12–26.

104. Stephen Nissenbaum, The Battle for Christmas, Vintage Books, New York, 1997, pp. 62, 109.

105. See Hannah Field, Playing with the Book: Victorian Movable Picture Books and the Child Reader, University of Minnesota Press, Minneapolis MN, 2019, pp. 25–58.

106. Andrew Lang, 'The Twelve Dancing Princesses', in The Red Fairy Book, Longmans, Green and Co., London and New York, 1890, pp. 1–12.

107. Oscar Wilde, The Complete Short Stories, ed. John Sloan, Oxford University Press, Oxford, 2020, pp. 77–8.

108. Joseph Bristow (ed.), Oscar Wilde and the Cultures of Childhood, Palgrave Macmillan, Basingstoke, 2017, p. 3.

109. Marcus Pfister, 'Evolution', www.marcuspfister.ch/evolution.htm (accessed 20 May 2022).

110. William Wordsworth, 'Ode on Intimations of Immortality from Recollections of Early Childhood', in The Complete Poetical Works of William Wordsworth, Macmillan, London, 1907, p. 359.

111. C.S. Lewis, The Lion, the Witch and the Wardrobe, Scholastic, New York, 1995, p. 19.

112. J.R.R. Tolkien, 'On Fairy-Stories', in The Monsters and the Critics and Other Essays, ed. Christopher Tolkien, HarperCollins, London, 2006, p. 153.

113. Maria Sachiko Cecire, Re-Enchanted: The Rise of Children's Fantasy Literature in the Twentieth Century, University of Minnesota Press, Minneapolis MN, 2019, pp. 119–24.

114. See, for instance, Stephanie Jones-Rogers, They Were Her Property: White Women as Slave Owners in the American South, Yale University Press, New Haven CT, 2019, pp. 2–10.

115. See Robin Bernstein, Racial Innocence: Performing American Childhood from Slavery to Civil Rights, New York University Press, New York, 2011.

116. Lang, The Red Fairy Book, pp. 6, 11.

117. See Ebony Elizabeth Thomas, The Dark Fantastic: Race and the Imagination from Harry Potter to the Hunger Games, New York University Press, New York, 2019.

118. Zetta Elliott, The Ghosts in the Castle, illus. Charity Russell, Rosetta Press, Brooklyn NY, 2017, p. 67.

119. Tracy Deonn, Legendborn, Margaret K. McElderry Books, New York, 2020, p. 471.

120. Inge Daniels, The Japanese House: Material Culture in the Modern Home, Berg, Oxford, 2010.

121. Some colleagues have highlighted the dangers of anonymity being breached, and, of course, participants' lives should never be endangered. However, rigid ethical protocols can also obstruct accessibility to data gathered and proper scrutiny of knowledge claims made.

122. See, for example, Haidy Geismar, 'Stone Men of Malekula on Malakula: An Ethnography of an Ethnography', Ethnos, vol. 74, no. 2, 2009, pp. 199–228, who discusses the impact of the Cambridge anthropologist John Layard's book Men of the Stone Age, based on his 1910s' fieldwork on Vanuatu, on the inhabitants of its islands many decades later.

123. See Inge Daniels, 'The Fame of Miyajima: Spirituality, Commodification and the Tourist Trade of Souvenirs', Ph.D. dissertation, University of London, 2001.

124. See Inge Daniels, 'The "Social Death" of Unused Gifts: Loss and Value in Contemporary Japan', *Journal of Material Culture*, vol. 14, no. 3, 2009, pp. 385–408, at pp. 388–9.

125. Ibid.

126. Inge Daniels, 'The Commercial and Domestic Rhythms of Japanese Consumption', in Elizabeth Shove et al. (eds), *Time, Consumption and Everyday Life: New Agendas and Directions*, Berg, Oxford, 2009, pp. 262–94.

127. Kula exchange consisted of seven different types of exchange depending on the level of closeness between the people involved. Ceremonial shells were exchanged as tokens of interpersonal relations between chiefs in unstable political environments; lesser functional items (including shells) were bartered between people who knew each other well. See Bronisław Malinowski, *Argonauts of the Western Pacific*, Routledge, London, 2014 (first published 1922).

128. Marcel Mauss, *The Gift: Expanded Edition*, trans. Jane I. Guyer, Hau Books, Chicago IL, 2016 (first published 1925).

129. The American anthropologist Anna Tsing argues that economic heterogeneity – the blurring of gifts and commodities – is at the base of capitalism. Attempts are constantly made to purify commodities by stripping them of gift-like relations, but this process can never be fully controlled and there are always contingencies. See Anna Tsing, *The Mushroom at the End of the World*, Princeton University Press, Princeton NJ, 2015.

130. Annette Weiner, 'Inalienable Wealth', *American Ethnologist* 12, 1985, pp. 210–27.

131. Nancy Munn, *The Fame of Gawa,* Cambridge University Press, Cambridge, 1986. The television documentary *Hunters of the South Seas* shows how the Kula Ring has fared after the islands became a destination on the luxury cruise tourism circuit. Tourist trade disrupts the 'traditional' Kula activities, but access to the cash economy has also loosened the power of 'Big Men'. See *Hunters of the South Seas*, Episode 3: *The Kula Ring*, dir. Will Lorimer, BBC 2, 2016.

132. A powerful spiritual force is inalienably linked with and wants to return to the donor, the community and the land. Failure to reciprocate will have spiritual repercussions such as bad luck. See Mauss, *The Gift*, pp. 65–75.

133. Mauss's *The Gift* was influenced by historical events. After the First World War when much of Europe was in ruins (many of Mauss's friends were killed), questions were raised about how such carnage and suffering could be avoided in the future: how could a society where people care for the common good be created?

134. George Serntedakis, '"Solidarity" for Strangers', *Etnofoor*, vol. 29, no. 2, 2017, pp. 83–98, discusses the rise of solidarity movements as an alternative to state provisioning in response to austerity and the refugee crisis in Greece.

135. James Carrier, 'Gifts in a World of Commodities: The Ideology of the Perfect Gift in American Society', *Social Analysis* 29, 1997, pp. 19–37.

136. R.L. Stirrat and Heiko Henkel, 'The Development Gift: The Problem of Reciprocity in the NGO World', *Annals of the American Academy of Political and Social Science* 554, 1997, pp. 66–80.

137. The impact of gifts of insecticide-treated mosquito nets on local net production in developing countries is one example; see Udi Beisel, 'Markets and Mutations: Mosquito Nets and the Politics of Disentanglement in Global Health', *Geoforum* 66, 2015, pp. 146–55.

138. See Jamie Cross and Alice Street, 'Anthropology at the Bottom of the Pyramid', *Anthropology Today*, vol. 25, no.4, 2009, pp. 4–9.

139. Cheryl Chapman and Cathy Ross, *Philanthropy: The City Story*, Press to Print, London, 2013; www.liverycompanies.info/livery-giving-report.pdf (accessed 22 May 2022).

140. See www.arkonline.org (accessed 25 March 2022).

141. Catherine Dolan, 'The New Face of Development', *Anthropology Today,* vol. 28, no. 4, 2012, pp. 3–7.

142. Eric Klinenberg, *Palaces for the People: How to Build a More Equal and United Society*, Vintage, London, 2018, pp. 219–20.

143. Ibid.

Further Reading

Chapter 1

John Barton, *A History of the Bible: The Book and Its Faiths*, Allen Lane, London, 2019.

Jeremy Black et al., *The Literature of Ancient Sumer*, Oxford University Press, Oxford, 2004.

Sarah Ruden (trans.), *The Aeneid. Vergil*, rev. edn, Yale University Press, New Haven CT, 2021.

Francesca Stavrakopoulou, *God: An Anatomy*, Picador, London, 2021.

Yunxiang Yan, 'Gifts', in Felix Stein (ed.), *The Cambridge Encyclopedia of Anthropology* online: http://doi.org/10.29164/20gifts (7 July 2020).

Chapter 2

Camillo Alessio Formigatti, *A Sanskrit Treasury: A Compendium of Literature from the Clay Sanskrit Library*, Bodleian Library Publishing, Oxford, 2019.

Stanley Frye (trans.), *The Sutra of the Wise and the Foolish (Mdo Mdzangs Blun), Or, Ocean of Narratives (Üliger-ün Dalai)*, 3rd edn, Library of Tibetan Works & Archives, Dharamsala, India, 2006.

Damien Keown, *Buddhism: A Very Short Introduction*, rev. edn, Oxford University Press, Oxford, 2013.

Andrew Skilton (ed. and trans.), *How the Nāgas Were Pleased*, Clay Sanskrit Library 39, New York University Press and JJC Foundation, New York, 2009.

Paul Williams et al., *Buddhist Thought: A Complete Introduction to the Indian Tradition*, 2nd edn, Routledge, New York, 2012.

Chapter 3

Simon Armitage (trans.), *Sir Gawain and the Green Knight*, Faber, London, 2007.

Geoffrey Chaucer, *The Canterbury Tales: A Selection*, trans. Colin Wilcockson (Middle English text with facing page translation), Penguin, London, 2008.

Christopher de Hamel, *Meetings with Remarkable Manuscripts*, Allen Lane/Penguin, London, 2016.

Frederica C.E. Law-Turner, *The Ormesby Psalter: Patrons & Artists in Medieval East Anglia*, Bodleian Library Publishing, Oxford, 2017.

Nicholas Perkins, *The Gift of Narrative in Medieval England*, Manchester University Press, Manchester, 2021.

Keith E. Small, *Qur'āns: Books of Divine Encounter*, Bodleian Library Publishing, Oxford, 2015.

Chapter 4

Francis Bacon, *The Major Works, including New Atlantis and the Essays*, ed. Brian Vickers, Oxford University Press, Oxford, 2008.

Ilana Ben-Amos, *The Culture of Giving: Informal Support and Gift-Exchange in Early Modern England*, Cambridge University Press, Cambridge, 2008.

Sir Thomas Elyot, *The Book Named the Governor*, ed. S.E. Lehmberg, Everyman's Library, Dent, London, 1962.

Felicity Heal, *The Power of Gifts: Gift-Exchange in Early Modern England*, Oxford University Press, Oxford, 2014.

Linda Levy Peck, *Court Patronage and Corruption in Early Stuart England*, Routledge, London, 1990.

Seneca, *Moral Essays III (De beneficiis)*, trans. J.W. Basore, Loeb Classical Library, Harvard University Press, Cambridge MA, 1975.

Chapter 5

Charlotte Brontë, *Selected Letters*, ed. Margaret Smith, Oxford University Press, Oxford, 2010.

William Craft and Ellen Craft, *Running a Thousand Miles for Freedom*, intr. Barbara McCaskill, Georgia University Press, Athens GA, 1999.

Charles Dickens, *A Christmas Carol & other Christmas Books*, ed. Robert Douglas-Fairhurst, Oxford University Press, Oxford, 2020.

Olaudah Equiano, *The Interesting Narrative of the Life of Olaudah Equiano, or Gustavus Vassa, the African: Written By Himself*, Hodder & Stoughton, London, 2021.

Katherine D. Harris, 'The Legacy of Rudolph Ackermann and Nineteenth-Century British Literary Annuals', *BRANCH: Britain, Representation, and Nineteenth-Century History*, ed. Dino Franco Felluga, https://branchcollective.org.

Jill Rappoport, *Giving Women: Alliance and Exchange in Victorian Culture*, Oxford University Press, Oxford, 2011.

Lucy Shaw, 'Wartime Fairy Tales', V&A blog, 18 December 2019, www.vam.ac.uk/blog/museum-life/wartime-fairy-tales.

Chapter 6

Robin Bernstein, *Racial Innocence*: *Performing American Childhood from Slavery to Civil Rights*, New York University Press, New York, 2011.

Maria Sachiko Cecire, *Re-Enchanted: The Rise of Children's Fantasy Literature in the Twentieth Century*, University of Minnesota Press, Minneapolis MN, 2019.

Hannah Field, *Playing with the Book: Victorian Movable Picture Books and the Child Reader*, University of Minnesota Press, Minneapolis MN, 2019.

Stephen Nissenbaum, *The Battle for Christmas*, Vintage Books, New York, 1997.

Ebony Elizabeth Thomas, *The Dark Fantastic: Race and the Imagination from Harry Potter to the Hunger Games*, New York University Press, New York, 2019.

J.R.R. Tolkien, 'On Fairy-Stories', in *The Monsters and the Critics and Other Essays*, ed. Christopher Tolkien, HarperCollins, London, 2006, pp. 109–61.

Chapter 7

Inge Daniels, *The Japanese House: Material Culture in the Modern Home,* Berg, Oxford, 2010.

Eric Klinenberg, *Palaces for The People: How to Build a More Equal and United Society*, Vintage, London, 2018.

Will Lorimer (dir.), *Hunters of the South*, Episode 3: *The Kula Ring,* BBC Worldwide 2016, https://learningonscreen.ac.uk/ondemand.

Michael Miller (dir.), *Poverty, Inc.*, Passion River Films, 2014.

Richard Sennett, *Together: The Rituals, Pleasures and Politics of Cooperation*, Penguin Books, London, 2012.

Anna Tsing, *The Mushroom at the End of the World: On the Possibility of Life in Capitalist Ruins*, Princeton University Press, Princeton NJ, 2015.

Contributors

Faith Binckes is Senior Lecturer in Modern and Contemporary Literature at Bath Spa University. Her recent publications include *Hannah Lynch (1859–1904): Irish Writer, Cosmopolitan, New Woman* (with Kathryn Laing, 2019) and *Women, Periodicals and Print Culture in Britain, 1890s–1920s: The Modernist Period* (co-ed., 2019).

Maria Sachiko Cecire is Associate Professor of Literature at Bard College. Her publications include *Re-Enchanted: The Rise of Children's Fantasy Literature in the Twentieth Century* (2019) and *Space and Place in Children's Literature, 1789 to the Present* (co-ed., 2015). She was the founding director of the Center for Experimental Humanities at Bard, is a National Project Scholar for the American Library Association's Great Stories Club for youth readers, and is currently a program officer for Higher Learning at the Mellon Foundation.

Inge Daniels is Professor of Anthropology at the Institute of Social and Cultural Anthropology, University of Oxford. Her publications include *The Japanese House* (2010) and *What Are Exhibitions For?* (2019).

Camillo A. Formigatti studied Classics, Indology and Tibetology. He was a research associate for the project 'In the Margins of the Text: Annotated Manuscripts from Northern India and Nepal', in Hamburg, and for the Sanskrit Manuscripts Project in Cambridge. He is currently a curator of South Asian manuscripts and information analyst for Oriental manuscripts at the Bodleian Libraries, Oxford.

Felicity Heal is an emeritus fellow of Jesus College, Oxford, and was a lecturer in History at the University of Oxford. She has published extensively on early modern British History, including a book on *The Power of Gifts: Gift-Exchange in Early Modern England* (2014).

Nicholas Perkins is Associate Professor and Tutor in English at St Hugh's College, University of Oxford. His publications include *Medieval Romance and Material Culture* (ed., 2015) and *The Gift of Narrative in Medieval England* (2021). He is the curator of the Bodleian's *Gifts and Books* exhibition (2023).

Francesca Stavrakopoulou is Professor of Hebrew Bible and Ancient Religion at the University of Exeter. Her recent publications include *God: An Anatomy* (2021) and *Life and Death: Social Perspectives on Biblical Bodies* (ed., 2021). Her media work includes programmes on BBC television and radio.

Picture Credits

Index

First published in 2023 by the Bodleian Library
Broad Street, Oxford OX1 3BG
www.bodleianshop.co.uk

ISBN: 978 1 85124 610 6

Front cover: detail from MS. Ashmole 45, fol. 2r, late 1520s. © Bodleian Library,
University of Oxford

Back cover: set of decorated platters, *c.*1590. © Ashmolean Museum,
University of Oxford

Publisher: Samuel Fanous
Managing Editor: Susie Foster
Editor: Janet Phillips
Picture Editor: Leanda Shrimpton
Designed and typeset by Dot Little in the Bodleian Library in 11/15pt Minion
Printed and bound by Printer Trento S.r.l. on 150gsm Gardamatt Art paper

British Library Catalogue in Publishing Data
A CIP record of this publication is available from the British Library